Patchwork Philosophy

Sylvia Charles

AuthorHouse™ UK
1663 Liberty Drive
Bloomington, IN 47403 USA
www.authorhouse.co.uk
UK TFN: 0800 0148641 (Toll Free inside the UK)
UK Local: 02036 956322 (+44 20 3695 6322 from outside the UK)

Because of the dynamic nature of the Internet, any web addresses or links contained in this book may have changed since publication and may no longer be valid. The views expressed in this work are solely those of the author and do not necessarily reflect the views of the publisher, and the publisher hereby disclaims any responsibility for them.

Any people depicted in stock imagery provided by Getty Images are models, and such images are being used for illustrative purposes only.
Certain stock imagery © Getty Images.

This book is printed on acid-free paper.

ISBN: 978-1-6655-9077-8 (sc)
ISBN: 978-1-6655-9076-1 (e)

Print information available on the last page.

Published by AuthorHouse 06/22/2021

authorHOUSE

Table of Contents

Acknowledgements

My thanks go to Dave Curtis, who very kindly gave me access to his collection of poetry named *"Poems from My Left Hand"*. These were originally all written by hand, as Dave was endeavouring to write with his left hand (being naturally right handed).

I would also like to thank the family of Terry Funnell for allowing me to use Terry's poetry.

Preface

For many years, I've had the idea of this book, and at last, I started putting my thoughts down on paper. Initially, I planned to call the book *The Earth Mother's Diary*, but on reflection, I thought that sounded rather twee. The next title I visualised was *Whoever Said Progress Was a One-Way Street?* but once again, I wasn't convinced this would create an impact, even though it was definitely my opinion. Eventually, due to the nature and content of my book, I hit upon *Patchwork Philosophy*, which seemed to fit the bill perfectly, so here it is.

I would stress that if some of my ideas are offensive to anyone, please don't be offended; they are purely the thoughts, ideas, and principles I try to live by.

This is the first book I have ever written (although I hope it won't be the last). Apart from my children and grandchildren, my passions and hobbies in life are gardening; crafting; homemaking, and baking. I really believe that over time an awful lot of babies have been thrown out with the bathwater in the name of progress, and that a return to some practices and ideologies of yesterday would greatly improve our lot today. I am also a Christian and hope this is reflected throughout this book.

When my son was small, his favourite book was called *What Do People Do All Day?* I wonder this myself sometimes, given all the labour-saving devices and technologies at our disposal, yet many people are still so stressed and busy, they have hardly any spare time at all. My question is, what do people do all day?

Please enjoy my book.

Readers can email me at sylviacharles135@btinternet.com.

Dedication

I'd like to dedicate this book to my daughter Jennie, who is a woman after my own heart, and my three beautiful granddaughters: Eloise, April, and Alice.

I'd also like to dedicate it to my maternal grandfather, James Henry and my paternal grandmother, Annie. James Henry was a wonderful influence in my life. He had a passion for gardening and making all sorts of useful (and sometimes not useful) items. When we were children, he would make us handkerchiefs from old white cotton flour bags. He made the most wonderful sweets: fudge, coconut ice, and toffee. He once made a wooden suitcase, which unfortunately was too heavy to lift (not one of his better ideas).

Grandma Annie was also a big part of my life; whenever we visited, she would usually be in her kitchen, wearing a three-quarter-length floral overall and making the most delicious goodies. Her favourites (and ours) were baked egg custard and coconut macaroons, along with many more.

As I got older, and after both grandparents passed away, I realised how much of them was in me. So as I carry on their passions of gardening, crafting, baking, and loving, my dedication and thanks go to them both.

My Child-Raising Tips

There are no hard and fast rules for successful child-rearing, but I firmly believe in following certain guidelines. We have no idea as parents if we are doing a good job whilst they are small; it is only when our children become adults that we can look at them and say, "I did a good job," or "I wish I had done more," or "I did my best." I guess doing our best is all we can do, and if we have done our best, there are no recriminations to be had. I have two children and six grandchildren; here are my top four tips on what I feel children need:

1. **Love.** Children need love in abundance at all stages of their lives, unconditional love that says, "I will always love you; I may not always like the things you do, but my love is and always will be unconditional." Children need to hear this on a regular basis.

2. **Affirmation.** Always be ready to say, "Well done," or "You really made me proud today," or "Thank you; you have been kind."

3. **No.** Children need to hear the word no. It isn't our job to say yes to things just to make us popular parents or to buy into peer pressure. I believe our role is to nurture physically, morally, and spiritually. We aren't supposed to be our children's best friend; in fact, proper parenting will sometimes make them think we are the enemy. I don't really like the expression "peer pressure"; it is no more than "keeping up with Joneses" for adults, it will only lead to dissatisfaction and envy. Teach them we can't have everything, and it is no bad thing to wait patiently for some things.

4. **Consequences.** I believe we should always teach our children that the choices they make, from very small choices to huge choices as they grow, will always bring consequences, either good or bad.

So my key words for successful child-rearing are love, affirmation, no, and consequences.

Also, parents get things wrong sometimes, so always be ready to apologise to your child if you know you did something wrong.

January

What I Love about January

I absolutely love the feeling that comes with a new year, the chance to make a fresh start, with twelve whole months stretching out ahead like a blank sheet of paper, just waiting to be written on. New goals to be set, new dreams to be dreamt. Needless to say, there will be trials, tribulations, and joys, but at this, the beginning of the year, they remain unknown.

I am an avid New Year's resolution maker, knowing I won't keep any for very long, but what a lovely time to reflect on things we would like to change or start, the person we'd like to become. Projects started but never finished can be unearthed, new ideas or hobbies to pursue. I just love the start of the New Year.

Epiphany commemorates when the three kings travelled to Bethlehem to find Jesus and offer Him gifts. The story is recorded in the Bible in Matthew 2:1-12.

With growing families, it can be difficult to manage to see everyone over the Christmas holiday so, several years ago, my daughter hit on the idea of having an Epiphany lunch. This seemed a brilliant idea to get the whole family together. We aren't a huge family, but our number would be a bit of a crowd in a home setting, so we usually meet at a pub or restaurant, where we can enjoy a meal, mingle, and have a good old chat. We really enjoy this as following all the Christmas and New Year celebrations, January can feel a bit flat, so it is something to look forward to.

Quote of the Month

Reputation is what folks think you are. Personality is what
you seem to be. Character is what you really are.
~~Alfred Armand Montapert (American author)

Poem of the Month

<u>Bubbling Water</u>

Bubbling water in my garden pond

Lurking goldfish waiting to respond

Sunbathing sparrows flicking deftly in the dust

The buzzing of bluebottles as they're swatted, thwacked and cussed

The sweet song of the robin as he flits around

The stealth of the grey squirrel as he searches the ground

The screech of the magpie as she feeds her young

The stare of the tabby as she sits quivering her tongue

All these lovely creatures surrounding me now

Out here in the garden and I'm wondering how

God made all this for us to gladden our eye

And that's just for starters, just look up at the sky.

—Dave Curtis (2004)

January To-Do's

➤ Send out thank-you notes for gifts or hospitality received at Christmas. The children can also make their own thank-you cards or write letters to send out.

➤ Take down all Christmas decorations by Twelfth Night (5 January). When packing away decorations, set aside the ones that haven't been used, and get rid of them. No use storing old or unwanted Christmas decorations (unless of course they are priceless having been made by the children).

➤ Save Christmas cards to make your own cards and gift tags for next year.

➤ If you are a pantomime fan, now is the time to book early for this year's panto to ensure you get good seats.

➤ Check out the shops for the stock of Seville marmalade oranges. They usually appear just after Christmas until late January.

➤ If you have bulbs in containers, move them to where you can see them. It is lovely to see snowdrops and aconites starting to grow.

Money-Saving Tips

➤ Whenever you cook or bake, make more than you need to ensure a supply for the freezer. I always make it a rule to use my largest pots and pans. When making mashed potatoes, for example, I do a huge panful and then with the leftovers make several small cheese-and-potato pies. You can add onions, mushrooms, or whatever you have handy; they freeze really well and are a great favourite comfort food. The children love them, and they make a great accompaniment to sausages, fish fingers, and so on. It is also lovely to have something savoury or sweet already prepared when visitors drop by unexpectedly.

➤ When I shop in the supermarket, I avoid buying things I can honestly live without. One such item is air fresheners. We read in the media that childhood asthma is on the increase, and some believe that the chemicals in air fresheners (and some candles) are a contributory factor. I say if you want your home to smell fresh, then throw open the windows and let the fresh air in on a daily basis.

Recipes of the Month

<u>Seville Orange Marmalade</u>

You will need preserving pan, large wooden spoon, muslin square, jam jars, waxed discs.

Ingredients

4 pints water, 2 lb Seville oranges, 1 lemon, 4 lb preserving sugar

Method

Put 4 pints water into preserving pan; cut fruit in half, squeeze juice out, and add to water. Next remove all pips and as much pith as possible from each shell and put in a muslin square, draped over a dish. Discard the lemon skins.

Cut each orange half into two, and shred finely with a sharp knife, adding shredded peel to the pan. Next, tie the muslin square securely into a bag and tie onto pan handle, immersing in liquid. Bring to boiling point and simmer for approximately one-and-a-half hours, until peel is soft.

While marmalade is simmering, weigh out sugar and put in ovenproof dish. Put two saucers in freezer ready for testing. Wash and dry jam jars and place on a tray ready to sterilise in a moderate oven. When peel is softened, heat oven to about 160 degrees (or gas mark 4), and put sugar in to warm for about 5-10 minutes. After removing sugar, place jam jars into oven to sterilise and leave for 15 minutes. Turn oven off but leave jars inside until required.

Remove muslin bag and leave to cool while slowly adding the warmed sugar to the pan and stirring well to make sure it is all completely dissolved. Take the muslin bag and squeeze over the pan until all the liquid and pectin have been squeezed out. This will take about 5 minutes. Make sure you keep squeezing until no more substance oozes out.

Stir well and bring pan to a rolling boil. Boil for 15 minutes, and then turn off the heat and test for setting point by placing a spoonful onto a saucer which has been in the freezer, place this in the fridge to cool. When cool, if setting point has been reached, a skin will form and crinkle when gently pushed. If not set, reboil for a further 10 minutes until a set is reached.

When set, remove from heat and stir in an ounce (2 tablespoons) of butter to disperse scum. Remove jars from oven. Leave marmalade to rest for 15 minutes. Pour into the clean sterilised jars. Cover jars immediately with a waxed disc and lid. Label jars when marmalade has gone cold.

Makes about 6 jars.

I often give marmalade, jams, and home baking as gifts; they are always much appreciated. For marmalade gifts, I use a hessian bag and also include a little marmalade recipe book I produced.

Marmalade Loaf

Ingredients

6 oz margarine, 2 oz sugar, 4 tablespoons golden syrup, 2 eggs, 5 oz marmalade, 10 oz self-raising flour, 1 teaspoon baking powder, 1 oz stem or crystallised ginger, finely chopped

Method

Cream together the margarine, sugar, and syrup. Gradually beat in the eggs. Stir in the marmalade, and fold in the flour, baking powder, and ginger. Put into a lined two-pound loaf tin and bake at 160 degrees for about 1 hour.

If you have a sweet tooth, this can be iced and decorated with orange zest or orange slices.

Home-made marmalade is delicious, so much tastier than shop bought, and I make several batches to ensure a good supply for use by myself, to give as gifts, and also to sell at craft fairs. Together with my recipe book, it's always a popular buy.

Marmalade Bread and Butter Pudding

Butter a pudding dish, butter 3-4 slices of white bread, and spread with marmalade. Cut into triangles and arrange in a dish. Scatter over a good handful of sultanas. Make a custard using 1 pint milk, 4 eggs, and 2 oz castor sugar (or use half a pint of milk to 2 eggs). Strain this over the bread and sprinkle with grated nutmeg. Let this stand for half an hour to allow the bread to soak up the custard. Bake in a moderate oven until custard is set. I love this served either hot or cold, with maybe a dash of single cream or yogurt.

February

What I Love about February

During this wonderful month, I have time to enjoy being indoors; no gardening jobs for me at this time of year. It's a great opportunity to browse gardening magazines and catalogues, and maybe plan some changes, or decide what plants to buy ready for the arrival of spring and the warmer weather. It's always a lovely time for me in the kitchen; with the marmalade usually made, it's now time to get on with the rhubarb jam. It's also a lovely time of year for those warming winter casseroles and comfort puddings.

Valentine's Day and Shrove Tuesday make lovely excuses for a celebration this month.

I think it's a shame to consign Valentine's Day to just romantic couples; instead, it's a lovely time to celebrate love in all its forms. You could make cards to send to family members, demonstrating how much you appreciate and love them. Children will love decorating and making their own cards too.

Shrove Tuesday: who doesn't love pancakes? Well, I know some people don't, but I adore pancakes and make loads, either savoury or sweet. I have a husband who would never eat a pancake, and I have a friend whose wife also doesn't enjoy, so some years I invite my friend over, and we share a mutual love of the delicious floppy pancakes, either with orange juice or smothered in golden syrup.

Quote of the Month

Giving is a joy if we do it in the right spirit. It all depends on whether
we think of it as "What can I spare?" or as "What can I share?"
—Esther York Burkholder

Poem of the Month

My granddad, James Henry, used to recite lots of poems to us as children; this was one
of our favourites:

Lament on the Death of Willie

Willie had a purple monkey climbing up a yellow stick,

And when he sucked the paint all off it made him deathly sick;

And in his latest hours he clasped that monkey in his hand,

And bade goodbye to earth and went to a better land.

Oh! No more he'll shoot his little sister with his little wooden gun;

And no more he'll twist the pussy's tail and make her yowl for fun.

The pussy's tail now stands up straight; the gun is laid aside;

The monkey doesn't jump around since little Willie died.

Julia Moore (1847-1920)

February To-Do's

➤ If you have children or grandchildren, start thinking and preparing for February half-term. Cinemas and museums are good for this time of the year, and many libraries offer children's activities. But don't cram the holiday with too many activities and treats; it's good for children to sometimes be bored, which provides an opportunity for their own imagination and creativity to kick in. If you are on a budget, then plan your own home activities (e.g., friends around for play and tea, baking day, art and craft day).

➤ Look out for the early forced rhubarb from Yorkshire to hit the shops; this is lovely, and I always buy as soon as I see it and make rhubarb jam, crumbles, and so on.

➤ Valentine's Day is a day for all to celebrate love. Make cards and chocolate goodies to give as gifts. No children around? Why not have a few friends around for a themed afternoon tea and maybe a DVD; be creative but celebrate.

Money-Saving Tips

➤ February can be a bit of a quiet month: Christmas is packed away and forgotten, spring seems a long way off, so why not spend a month being creative? I collect different size jars, wash them well, and store them away, ready to use as gift containers. Jam jars are lovely to decorate and fill with a variety of things: sweets, biscuits, bath bombs, almost anything, and then decorate the jar with ribbons and labels. This home-made gift not only saves you money but is really appreciated, as it demonstrates time and effort by the giver.

➤ If you can knit, crochet, or sew, why not start a stash of small gift items (e.g., scarves, gloves, cushions)? I knit and crochet endless numbers of cotton dishcloths; prettily packaged, they make a useful and environmentally friendly gift. The list is endless, and you have a supply of gifts ready to give out.

➤ My supermarket item to avoid for saving money this month is fabric softener (unless you live in a really hard water area). I find it completely unnecessary and never use it. I don't think you can beat the fragrance of washing hung out on a line and blown about on a windy day, a lovely free smell. But I know that some areas really do need help with hard water.

I am including my pattern for knitted dishcloths.

Knitted Dishcloth Pattern

Materials

Balls of 100 per cent cotton double knitting, plus pair of 4.1/2 knitting needles.

Cast on 51 stitches.

Work 8 rows moss stitch (knit 1 purl 1 on every row)

Continue in garter stitch, keeping 8 stitches either side in moss stitch to form a border.

When work is an approximate square, work 8 more rows in moss stitch then cast off. Work in any loose ends.

These are washable and extremely hardwearing, and save buying disposable cloths, much kinder to the environment.

Pegs in a tub and dishcloths on line

Washing on clothesline, by David Charles

Recipes of the Month

Rhubarb and Ginger Jam

You will need preserving pan, large wooden spoon, jam jars, waxed discs.

Ingredients

3 lb. prepared forced Yorkshire rhubarb, 3 lb preserving sugar, juice only of 3 lemons, 1 jar stem ginger in syrup (300 g)

Method

Cut rhubarb into 1-inch pieces and layer into a preserving pan with a covering of sugar over each layer (this can be done and left overnight). Next day, add lemon juice and simmer slowly until soft.

Then add remainder of sugar (which has been warmed in a low oven) and add drained, chopped-up ginger.

When all sugar is dissolved, bring up to a boiling point until setting point is reached (see marmalade recipe for setting point and sterilising jars).

Add knob of butter to disperse any scum and put into jars, cover with a waxed disc and lid immediately, and label when cold.

Note: After visiting the Rhubarb Shed in Yorkshire, I couldn't find a recipe for rhubarb and ginger jam, so made this up myself; it works really well. It is lovely to use as a jam or as a base for a crumble or in cakes and buns. I love a couple of dollops in Greek yoghurt as a dessert.

Pancake Batter

8 oz plain flour, pinch salt, 2 eggs, half and half milk and water to mix to a smooth batter. Leave batter to stand a while and then make your pancakes; make sure pan is really hot, and don't use too much sunflower oil. Stack them up as you make them; I always put a layer of baking parchment in between and keep warm. Serve with a variety of toppings (e.g., oranges, sugar, syrup, chocolate, or salted caramel spread). Any leftover ones can be frozen and used for savoury dishes as well. Pancakes make a good substitute for pasta in a lasagne.

Spinach, Mushroom, and Ricotta Pancake Filling

Ingredients

Pancakes, 1 bag fresh or frozen spinach, 1 oz butter or olive oil, 1 medium onion diced, 8 oz mushrooms thinly sliced, 1 oz plain flour, 1 tub ricotta cheese, salt, pepper, handful of breadcrumbs mixed with same amount of grated cheese.

Method

Wash the spinach well, put in a saucepan with 1 tablespoon water, and cook for about 5 minutes, until wilted. Drain well, chop finely.

Melt the butter or olive oil, fry the onion until softened, stir in the mushrooms, and cook for a few minutes until browned.

Sprinkle flour over and mix well, cook for a further 1-2 minutes, add the tub of ricotta cheese and mix well, stir until thickened, then add spinach and seasoning.

Spread each pancake with some of the mixture down the centre, then roll up and place in an ovenproof dish. Melt 1 oz butter, pour over the pancakes, then cover with the breadcrumb-and-cheese mixture.

Bake in oven at 170 (or gas mark 5) for 15-20 minutes, until browned and heated through.

If using freshly made pancakes, any leftover ones maybe frozen.

Barney's Roasted Rhubarb and Custard Cake

I have no idea where this recipe came from; I may have found it in a magazine, but it is delicious and makes a lovely large, and extremely moist, cake which doubles as a pudding.

Ingredients

400g rhubarb, 50g caster sugar, ½ teaspoon of ground ginger, 250g butter or margarine, 150g pot ready-made custard (use shop bought, as home-made custard doesn't work in this cake), 250g self-raising flour, 1 teaspoon baking powder, 4 large eggs, 1 teaspoon vanilla extract, 250g caster sugar, icing sugar for dusting.

Method

Heat oven to 200/fan 180 (or gas no. 6)

Rinse and trim rhubarb, cut into half-inch pieces, then place in shallow dish or baking tray, cover with 50g sugar and ginger, and toss together.

Cover with foil and roast for 15 minutes, then remove foil, shake tray, and roast for a further 5 minutes; drain off juice, and leave to cool.

Grease a 23 cm loose-bottomed cake tin; heat oven to 180/fan 160/gas no. 4.

Reserve 3 tablespoons of custard then beat the rest of the custard together with butter, flour, baking powder, eggs, vanilla, and sugar until smooth and creamy.

Spoon 1/3 of the mix into the tin, add some rhubarb, then dot with 1/3 more cake mix, spread out as well as you can. Top with some more rhubarb, then spoon over remaining cake mix; don't worry about it being too smooth. Scatter the rest of the rhubarb over the batter, then dot the remaining custard over in random dessertspoons full; don't smooth out but leave a rough surface.

Bake for 40 minutes until risen and golden, then cover with foil and bake for a further 20 minutes until a skewer inserted comes out clean.

Cool in tin then dredge with icing sugar.

Stew and Dumplings

Who doesn't love a good old-fashioned stew and dumplings? There are so many variations on this, I wouldn't write a set recipe. It's always best to use a good-quality stewing steak, or shin beef, or whatever is your favourite cut. I put the cubed meat in a large saucepan for the top of the stove or a large casserole, if I am using the oven. Then in go a variety of vegetables; the usual ones are onions, carrots, swede, or turnip, whatever is your choice or whatever you have available. I also use leeks and parsnips. I use a vegetarian beef stock cube and add this to the meat and vegetables; I never thicken a stew. Cook on the top or in the oven; long and slow is the best way, whichever method you chose. Make dumplings using beef or vegetable suet, flour, salt, and water to mix. The recipe for dumplings can always be found on the box of suet. I add dried parsley instead of salt. Divide your dumpling mix into 6 or 8, and drop on the top of the simmering stew and cover. They will take about 20 minutes and are ready when they are golden and risen. I always make a huge pan of stew with at least 8 dumplings because it freezes really well, and it's lovely to have some ready meals for busy days.

Sausage Casserole

This is a real favourite of mine, and if cooking for one or two people, there will be plenty left over to freeze. In a large frying pan, brown the sausages; when browned, add chopped onions and let them soften Then I add a carrot chopped small, a tin of drained butter beans or chickpeas, tin of chopped tomatoes, and a vegetable stock cube dissolved in about half a pint of hot water. The butter beans thicken the casserole really well; use 2 tins or just multiply your ingredients, depending on how much you want to make. When everything has reached boiling point, simmer with a lid on for about 45 minutes, stirring occasionally. Goes lovely with some creamy mashed potatoes.

Barbara's Toffee Squares

This recipe was given to me years ago by my friend Barbara. Before she moved to Australia, this was our favourite treat to enjoy with a coffee.

Ingredients

Base: 5oz self-raising flour, 2oz sugar, 4oz margarine

Toffee filling: 4oz butter, 4oz soft brown sugar, 2 tablespoons golden syrup, 1 tin condensed milk (405g)

Topping: 6oz melted chocolate

Method

Cream margarine and sugar; fold in the flour. Press into a greased and lined tin and bake at gas mark 5 or 170 fan for 15 minutes. Leave to cool. Place all toffee ingredients into a pan and heat until boiling; reduce the heat and simmer for 5 minutes, stirring continuously. Pour over the cooled base. When set, cover with the melted chocolate. Leave until cold then cut into squares.

Fudgematic Delight

This popular recipe has many variations, but this is how I make it. The name was the idea of my son; when he was small, he asked if I could make some more "of that fudgematic delight."

Ingredients

6oz chocolate, 4oz butter, 1 large tin condensed milk (405g), 10oz rich tea or digestive biscuits. Topping: 6oz melted chocolate

Method

Melt the chocolate, butter, and condensed milk together. Stir into the crushed biscuits. Spread into a lined and greased tin, and chill. When set, cover with melted chocolate. Leave until cold then cut into squares.

Both these recipes make lovely gifts for Valentine's Day. In the past, I have used specially shaped cutters to stamp out heart shapes, then some lucky person gets to eat all the leftover trimmings.

They also make lovely chocolate Easter treats; cut into small squares, place in clear cellophane bags, and tie with ribbon.

Spring picture of trees and crocus

March

What I Love about March

This is the month when spring officially starts, on March 20th. It is usually when my gardening year starts. I do know some professional gardeners, and very keen amateurs, who say you can garden every day of the year regardless of the weather, but I don't fall into this category. March for me is the start of another year of pruning, planting, and eating out in my garden and generally enjoying the outdoors whenever possible.

So between March and, say, October, I may feel compelled to include some gardening hints, so watch out for them if you are a gardener.

This month is also Mothering Sunday.

Quote of the Month

One who loves is borne on wings; he runs and is filled with joy, he is free and unrestricted. Love feels no burden and counts up no toil; it aspires to do more than its strength allows, It does not plead impossibility; but considers that it may do, and can do, all things.

Thomas á Kempis (1380-1471)

Poem of the Month

Anyway

People are often unreasonable, illogical and self-centred;

Forgive them anyway

If you are kind, people may accuse you of selfish, ulterior motives; Be kind anyway

If you are successful, you will win some false friends and some true enemies;

Succeed anyway.

If you are honest and frank, people may cheat you;

Be honest and frank anyway.

What you spend years building, someone could destroy overnight;

Build anyway.

If you find serenity and happiness, they may be jealous;

Be happy anyway.

The good you do today, people will often forget tomorrow;

Do good anyway.

Give the world the best you have, and it may never be enough;

Give the world the best you've got anyway.

—Mother Teresa

I read recently that this poem was not actually written by Mother Theresa, but she loved it, and it was pinned on the wall of the orphanage where she worked.

March To-Dos

I think the foregoing quote and poem are absolutely perfect for this month, when we celebrate Mothering Sunday.

➢ So make plans for what sort of celebration you will be part of on Mothering Sunday. If you have a mum, what will you do to spoil her? If you don't have a mum, could you perhaps buy an ethical gift in her memory?

➢ If you are not part of any particular celebration, perhaps you can get a few friends together for a special afternoon tea. Be creative; there is always something you can do to make the day different, and we all need a treat every now and then.

➢ Maybe visit a garden centre for ideas for the coming year.

➢ If there are children around, let them make cards and gifts; don't be tempted to overspend. This day is about love and celebration, not about expensive gifts.

➢ Depending on when Easter falls, start to make plans for Easter holidays, entertaining (egg hunts for the children), and catering plans if you are inviting family/friends around. Also, if you are a baker, check your store cupboard to make sure you have all the ingredients for making a traditional simnel cake and other Easter goodies.

➢ If you are a traditionalist (or a lady of a certain age), March is usually the time of year when thoughts turn to a good spring clean. I admit I like to stick to giving the house a good going over at least twice a year (spring and November, to be ready for Christmas). By this, I mean maybe taking curtains down, taking stock of any redecorating jobs, clearing out cupboards and drawers, and generally a good taking stock of our home.

In My Garden

➢ This is the month when, if weather allows, roses should be pruned hard and fed, ready for their first flowering.

➢ It's also time to prune any hydrangeas (I have several). Deadhead all the previous year's brown flower heads, and prune bushes to your required size/shape.

➢ This is also a good month for clearing out all last year's dead growth around perennials, but take care not to damage any new shoots emerging.

➢ I enjoy clearing and sweeping all hard areas, getting rid of moss and giving borders and tubs a general feed, using home-made compost spread as a mulch or any general organic commercial fertilizer.

➤ The greenhouse also benefits from a good clearing out and washing down; make sure all seed trays are clean and ready for sowing seeds of herbs, vegetables, flowers, and so on.

Money-Saving Tips

➤ Supermarket shopping: This month, I highlight all the disposable products for cleaning, which I personally feel I could well do without. For cleaning windows, there are several products available, most of which come in plastic containers (although they may be recyclable, they are best avoided if at all possible). I have always managed to clean my windows with a good old-fashioned window leather and a soft, clean fluffy duster. This saves money and helps the environment.

➤ If you have a greenhouse or a cold frame, it's a good time to peruse plant catalogues and buy plug plants, which are much, much cheaper than the ready-to-plant annuals and perennials found in garden centres. Grow on until large enough to transplant, and plant out when all frosts are over.

Recipes of the Month

With Mothering Sunday in mind, I don't think you can go wrong with a traditional Victoria sponge. I give the basic recipe below; it's very versatile and can be adapted into all sorts of different cakes, buns, or puddings.

Basic Ingredients

6oz margarine, 6oz castor sugar, 3 large eggs, 6oz self-raising flour, 1 teaspoon baking powder, 1 teaspoon vanilla extract

Method

Cream butter and sugar, add eggs and vanilla, then fold in flour. Divide into 2 greased and lined cake tins (8-inch) and bake at gas mark 5 for 20/25 minutes, until firm to the touch and golden brown. When cooled, the cakes can be sandwiched together with jam or buttercream, and the top sprinkled with castor sugar.

You will note the combination of 6oz of everything to 3 eggs; this can either be doubled or multiplied, depending on how much mixture you need (e.g., 4 oz of everything to 2 eggs, or 8 oz of everything to 4 eggs; the choice is yours). For chocolate mix, substitute a quarter of the flour with cocoa powder, or for coffee, add 1 or 2 tablespoons of coffee essence (camp coffee).

You can choose to make 1 large cake or about 18 cupcakes (placed in a large dish, it can be used as a pudding). Be inventive with additions like dried fruit, marmalade, coconut, golden syrup, or anything else you fancy.

If you want to ice your cake or buns, just mix a quantity of icing sugar with warm water to a stiff consistency and spread, using a warm knife (keep dipping in hot water for a smooth finish).

Peppermint Squares

Another family favourite, particularly loved by my brother. I usually make this for him instead of an Easter egg.

Ingredients

Base: 4oz butter, 2 teaspoons cocoa powder, 2½oz cornflakes, crushed,

4oz self-raising flour, 3oz soft brown sugar

Topping: 8oz icing sugar, 1½ tablespoons hot water, ½ teaspoon peppermint essence, and a drop of green food colouring.

Method

Base: Melt butter, and stir into the dry ingredients. Press into a greased and lined Swiss roll-size tin, and bake at gas mark 4 or 160 fan for 20 minutes. Set aside to cool.

Topping: Combine all the icing ingredients, and spread over the base; using a hot knife helps. Leave to set, then cover with 7oz melted chocolate. When set, cut into squares.

Easter Biscuits

This recipe was passed to me by my mother-in-law.

Ingredients

8oz plain flour, 4oz margarine, 6oz castor sugar, 3oz currants (I substitute sultanas), 1 egg, plus a little milk if necessary

Method

Rub the margarine into the flour. Add sugar and currants (or sultanas). Mix to a stiff dough, with egg and milk if required. Roll out and cut into rounds. Place on greased trays, and bake for 15 minutes at gas mark 4 or 160 fan, until nice and golden.

April

What I Love about April

Whilst March gives us a hint that spring is approaching, I feel April shouts out that spring has arrived. We've already had the pleasure of the early bulbs (aconites, snowdrops, etc.), followed by the daffodils and primroses, and now the tulips and other early perennials are flowering freely. The trees are beginning to show a definite covering of greenery, so fresh, so bright, and jobs in the garden become a reality and an enormous pleasure once more (for me, anyway).

Easter

For Christians, Easter is such an important time; we follow the Easter story through Holy Week to the crucifixion and resurrection of Jesus.

Quote of the Month

I am not what I ought to be.
I am not what I want to be.
I am not what I hope to be in another world.
But still, I am not what I once used to be.
And by the Grace of God, I am what I am.
—John Newton

Article of the Month

A Woman's Place

I have been a full time Mum for nearly five years and would like to (politely) dispel the commonly held view by those working mothers who have cause to comment on my domestic arrangements that I am either a) mad b) exceedingly rich or c) missing out on something.

It is true that motherhood envelops us in exhilaration and despair; pride and shame; energy and exhaustion; laughter and tears ... so I admit that to some, making a choice to walk this path on a daily (sometimes hourly!) basis, can indeed, seem like insanity!

But, opting to grow and change by these experiences is only part of the decision to be at home full time. I wanted to make a concrete commitment to my baby that said "I love you. I will always be here for you." Because 75% of all information a child, in his early years, absorbs is taken in through his eyes, I figured the most effective way to impress upon him my commitment was for him to see me physically—constantly. He knows I will always be there for him, for he sees I am always there for him. There is, then, a method to my madness!!

Also, I often hear working mothers say that they would love to be at home with their babies if only they could afford not to work, which infers that I can, when in reality I have chosen to provide me, rather than goods. Our standard of living hasn't nose-dived drastically by me not working, it's just remained static, which doesn't rate highly in a society that brainwashes us into believing we must be ever on the upward—financially and materially.

Comparing my own experiences of working full time in a well paid job pre-baby, and my life now, my satisfaction and all round feeling of well being is far, far greater now than then. The qualities, intellect and motivation I need to search for to raise my child successfully is a more stimulating, mind and soul expanding process than any I ever found outside the home. To teach daily about love, forgiveness, anger, compassion and dozens more necessary life skills is no small task and I, personally, could never put a price tag on its importance.

My baby starts school in September and it is the speed at which this time at home has passed that, for me, reinforces the feeling that I have missed nothing and gained everything. I have shared every single day of my son's life and, therefore, have been able to witness all the sweetness of his nature unfolding first hand.

Children live their lives whether we are there or not. They speak, laugh, cry, feel and think as the moment dictates, and the blessings and opportunities to nurture are there for those who are with them at that specific time.

My son's babyhood years have passed now, forever. I treasure photographs, scribbled drawings and boxes of too-small clothing to remind me how he has grown and changed, but the most precious treasure of all is that which is unseen, thousands of special spoken and silent acts I have shared with my child, stored safely in my memory and, if missed as they happen, can never be recaptured.

All this passion and sentiment has not, I assure you, left me devoid of all personal ambition. One day I will pursue a fulfilling career, travel, study, throw lavish dinner parties and own a Marks and Spencer charge card! But whoever started the rush? I think I'll wait, for it'll all be there tomorrow. For now, I am happy to know that this woman's very personal place is in the home.

—Jennie Wright

(This article was written in 1996 by my daughter for the NCT newsletter and reproduced with her permission.)

April To-Dos

- ➤ Shop for gifts for Easter (e.g., eggs or other goodies).
- ➤ Make or buy Easter greeting cards.
- ➤ Decorate an Easter tree.
- ➤ Make a traditional simnel cake.
- ➤ Find out what services are being held at your local church; there are often activities for children at church or maybe your local library.
- ➤ Don't forget to let your children know and understand why we are celebrating Easter; the chocolate goodies, chicks, and bunnies are an extra treat.
- ➤ Make an Easter wreath for the front door.
- ➤ Plan entertaining for family and friends.

In the Garden

- ➤ Sow hardy annuals and perennials (either directly in the ground or greenhouse).
- ➤ Primulas and polyanthus are an inexpensive way of adding some instant colour in front of borders or in pots or tubs.
- ➤ Deadhead spring bulbs (but leave the leaves to die back naturally).
- ➤ Sow sunflower seeds; children love to plant these and watch them grow.
- ➤ Hoe your garden regularly; it saves time weeding later.

Money-Saving Tips

So what do I think I can do without from the supermarket this month? Well, not exactly do without, but use much less frequently: cling film.

There was a time I used quite a lot of this to cover food in the fridge, but I came to realise that the old way, what my mother used to do, (once she became the owner of a fridge) was to cover items with a saucer or a plate, works just as well. However, there are times when cling film is a necessity, such as when I am making vanilla slices (I'll include the recipe below).

I also try and use tin foil as sparingly as possible. I wrap sandwiches in greaseproof paper or bags, and to cover a pan in the oven, I use a roasting tray with a lid.

Recipe of the Month

<u>Vanilla Slices</u>

The first time I made these, I was so pleased at how easy they were and how delicious they were. All you need is a sheet of puff pastry, a pint of thick home-made custard, and icing sugar.

First, lay out the puff pastry on a floured board and mark into small oblongs; bake these in a hot oven and when baked slice in half. After making a pint of thick custard, line a Swiss roll tin with cling film and pour the cooled custard in. Leave to set, and then flip out onto a board and cut into slices the same size as your puff pastry oblongs. Sandwich together, spread with glacé icing (icing sugar made with hot water), and spread using a warm knife.

Absolutely delicious.

<u>Lemonies (as Opposed to Brownies)</u>

Ingredients

8oz castor sugar; 6oz plain flour; 1 teaspoon baking powder; 4oz butter or margarine; 2 large eggs; 4 small lemons (zest and juice); 2oz white chocolate chips

Icing: 1 cup icing sugar; remainder of lemon zest mixed with remaining lemon juice

Method

Heat oven to 170 fan or no. 5 gas mark; grease and line Swiss roll-size baking tin. Grate lemon zest and squeeze juice.

Beat butter and sugar together; add eggs gradually; add flour, baking powder, and chocolate chips. Add lemon zest, but save some for icing mix, and then add lemon juice, saving some for icing mix. Pour into baking tin, and bake for 20-25 minutes, until browned (be careful not to overbake).

Leave to cool completely, then prick over top with fork or cocktail stick and drizzle over icing mix, then cut into squares. Delicious.

Coconut Bars

Another scrumptious chocolate recipe, perfect for a coffee morning or makes another lovely treat as a gift, or just to munch and enjoy yourself.

Ingredients

Base: 5 oz plain flour, 4 oz sugar, 3 oz desiccated coconut, 1 tablespoon cocoa, 6 oz butter, 1 egg, 1 teaspoon vanilla extract.

Topping: 6 oz icing sugar, 2 tablespoons cocoa powder, 1 oz margarine, 1-2 tablespoons hot water. Additional desiccated coconut for topping.

Method

Melt the butter and stir into the base dry ingredients; add the egg and vanilla extract, press into a greased and lined oblong tin, and bake at gas mark 4 or fan 160 for 20 minutes. Cool and then cream the topping ingredients together; spread evenly over the base, and sprinkle liberally with the coconut. Cut into squares.

May

What I Love about May

May is so full of promise; this is one of my two favourite months of the year (the other is September). Everything outdoors, whether in the countryside, gardens, or parks, looks so new, vibrant, bright, and fresh; leaf and bud are uncurling everywhere, with promises of the forthcoming summer display. I absolutely love eating outdoors; and will eat most meals outside, whenever possible. For me, the anticipation of what will follow is so exciting. It's a month full of hope and encouragement.

Quotes of the Month

You are never too old to set another goal or to dream a new dream.
—C S Lewis

You can't go back and change the beginning but you can
start where you are and change the ending.
—C S Lewis

Life is 10% what happens to us, and 90% how we react to it.
—usually attributed to Charles Swindoll or Dennis Kimbro

Poem of the Month

Our World

Our world is a magnificent place, it's just like a star that shines in space.

But when we hurt our world or litter, it's just like a lime that tastes so bitter.

Also, when we use a plane, it lets out gas, which is insane!

So now you know what not to do, let's start to look at something new.

Let's look at how we can be a bit more green, let's pull together to make a team.

We can recycle all the things we use, like bottle tops and worn-out shoes,

Plastic cups and rubber bands, lollypop sticks and old bean cans.

So, thank you all for listening, now let our world be glistening.

—Alice Wright J2X

May To-Dos

By this time, I'm usually still on with my unfinished indoor spring cleaning. However, it's nice to get outside, weather permitting, and have a good clean-up outdoors too: clearing all paths and patios, washing old plant pots and seed trays, cleaning outside paintwork and windows, washing garden furniture, and so on; the list is endless. I aspire to complete my inside and outside cleaning by the end of this month, with a view to a long lazy summer (hopefully).

May in My Garden

Most days, I try and get in the garden to actually do some work. I can positively spend hours just meandering around and enjoying everything that's blooming, so I have to make sure I really do get stuck in. Hoeing and weeding are my top priority, also keep on trimming back and dead-heading early spring flowering bulbs and plants (remember, leave the foliage on bulbs to die back naturally). Keeping borders tidy allows the early and late summer plants to flourish.

If you have flowers or shrubs in containers, make sure you feed them regularly. I use a general liquid fertiliser (diluted) and feed all tubs and containers once a week (except the ones that are winter flowering; I start to feed these around the end of autumn).

Money-Saving Tips

Using up leftovers can really save you a lot of money. In the past, I admit I have wasted food (most people would admit to having done so), but with some thought, it is possible to avoid wasting good food, and by being inventive with leftovers, you can create mouth-watering meals.

Let's start with bread; who hasn't had stale bread left in the bottom of the bread bin? These days, I make my own bread, and to avoid wasting any, I slice it up and freeze a few slices per bag; this ensures fresh bread until the very last slice (you can do the same with shop-bought bread). If I do have some I haven't used and it's getting a bit stale, I stick it in the liquidizer and make breadcrumbs for freezing. Breadcrumbs mixed with grated cheese make a brilliant topping for all sorts of recipes. I'll include one or two of my favourites later on.

Now for vegetables: Every Friday, I have a box of vegetables delivered by Riverford Organic. It's wonderful to have lovely fresh veggies delivered to the doorstep, and it has introduced me to vegetables I would never have chosen from the supermarket, such as fennel, kohlrabi, and Swiss chard, to name a few.

By the end of the week, I inevitably have some leftovers, which are almost ready to be discarded, but not in my kitchen. As my veggie box is delivered on a Friday, I always use that day to make soup. This consists of anything which is left over, and if it needs something to top it up, I have my new box to hand. Without fail, summer or winter, I always have a bowl of home-made vegetable soup for lunch or tea. There is no better way of making sure you are getting a good variety of veg; you would never be able to eat the same amount on a plate as in a bowl of soup. It is also a good way of getting vegetables down your children.

When my children were small, they would ask, "What is it?"

I would always reply, "It's your favourite," and it worked (most of the time). I have included some soup recipes and tips.

Leftover meat: There are lots of ways to use up leftover roast joints. My mother-in-law showed me how to use up a small amount of roast beef: chop fairly small and place in blender with 2-3 oz melted butter, a tablespoon of horseradish sauce, or mustard. Season with salt and pepper. This makes a lovely potted beef sandwich filling.

Pork can be minced and made into burgers; you could mix this with a packet of made up stuffing mix to bulk out and maybe bind with a beaten egg.

I also mince lamb and use it to make a moussaka if there is enough or burgers with added chopped mint.

A roast chicken carcass is brilliant for making chicken soup.

It is so extremely satisfying knowing you have created dishes from food that otherwise would have loitered in the fridge before being discarded.

Recipes of the Month

<u>Chicken and Broccoli Bake</u>

This recipe has been in our family for years; it was originally given to my sister by her niece, who lives in Canada. It is a firm favourite and one I always use for large family gatherings.

Ingredients

4 cooked chicken breasts, 1 head of broccoli, 2 cans of condensed chicken soup, 4 teaspoons mayonnaise, 2 teaspoons mild curry powder, grated cheese, and breadcrumbs

Method

Butter a large ovenproof casserole, cut chicken breasts into small pieces, and cover base. Spread over the cooked broccoli. In a bowl, mix the 2 cans of condensed soup with the mayonnaise and curry powder (you can add a small amount of milk or single cream). In another bowl, mix a couple handfuls of breadcrumbs with the same amount of grated cheese. Cover the dish, and add a little more grated cheese on top, with a sprinkling of parsley. Bake in a hot oven, fan 180 or gas mark 6 for about 30-40 minutes.

This recipe is marvellous; I can happily eat leftovers, cold, with a salad. It is very versatile; you can either halve or multiply the ingredients for smaller or larger gatherings.

I sometimes substitute salmon fillets for the chicken and use asparagus (fresh or frozen) instead of broccoli. When using fish, I substitute condensed celery soup instead of chicken. But the choice is yours; you can mix and match any meat or fish, vegetable, or type of soup to suit what you have available.

Smoked Mackerel Pate

I love smoked mackerel but much prefer to eat it as a pate. This recipe is so easy and makes the mackerel go much further.

Ingredients

1 packet of smoked mackerel (skinned), 1 large handful of brown or white breadcrumbs, 1 tablespoon freshly chopped parsley or 1 teaspoon dried parsley, juice of half a lemon, 1-2 tablespoons mayonnaise or crème fraiche, 2 teaspoons Dijon mustard, 2oz melted butter, salt, and pepper

Method

Place all the ingredients in a bowl and mix thoroughly; if you prefer a finer texture at this stage, tip the contents into a liquidizer and blitz.

This is delicious served with warm toast or some nice savoury cheese biscuits.

Again, versatility is my keyword; you can make pate with any tinned fish, like salmon or tuna. It's such a good way of making a little go a long way and is something that can be prepared in advance if you are entertaining.

Bakewell Tart

Of all the dishes I bake, this surely has to be my family's favourite. I have been making Bakewell tarts for years; no family gathering would be complete without one.

Ingredients

Pastry: 6 oz self-raising flour, 3 oz butter, cold water to mix

Filling: any jam, although raspberry is the traditional choice

Topping: 2oz margarine, 2oz sugar, 1 egg, 1oz ground almonds, 1oz self-raising flour, 1 teaspoon vanilla extract, 2 teaspoons almond extract

Method

Make pastry and line a round flan dish. Spread thinly with jam of choice. Beat together the topping ingredients and spread over the jam. Bake at gas mark 5 or 170 fan for 10 minutes, then reduce to gas mark 4 or fan 160 for a further 20 minutes, or until golden.

Before baking, you can scatter flaked almonds on top, or if you prefer, bake as above and ice with glacé icing and decorate with cherries and flaked almonds.

The Lavender House

This is what I call my summerhouse, which sits at the bottom of my garden. It is where I pursue my love of all things crafty. Although I have heating and lighting installed, it is as summer approaches that I tend to spend much more time working away. I can open the doors and enjoy the finer weather and also have my little dog for company, he loves to nestle down in his basket, venturing out to chase the odd bird or squirrel.

Although I love a huge variety of crafts, I could never class myself as being terribly artistic. Some crafts I try once and abandon; I was never a great success at glass painting or candle making, but give me some fabric, ribbons, lace, and buttons, and my imagination will go into overdrive. I never think of an item to make and then obtain the materials; I just collect all fabrics, the more vintage the better, and then think, "now, what would this look good as?" I search my ribbon stash and button box for bits and pieces to adorn what I make.

I make a huge assortment of fabric items (e.g., peg bags, shopping bags, laundry bags, toilet bags, aprons, cushion covers, tablecloths; the list is endless). I also make lots of lavender products with lavender from my garden: lavender bags, lavender and sea salt foot soak, lavender soap. I produced a lovely little recipe leaflet with ideas for making cakes and biscuits using culinary lavender, these sell well at craft fairs. Lots of the things I make I give away as gifts.

Door wreaths are something I love, and not just for Christmas; I make myself an Easter wreath, summer wreath, autumn wreath. I just love a decorated front door.

My belief is that most people have a creative streak within them; it's just a matter of identifying what form yours happens to take; making things gives me an enormous amount of satisfaction, so why not try something for yourself? You may well be surprised at the result.

Summerhouse

Summer fabric flower garland

Easter wreath

Summer flowers

June

What I Love about June

Summer is here. This is where I hope, optimistically, that my spring cleaning and outdoor jobs have all been completed. If I have failed (which often is the case), then here is where one of my mottos kicks in: "Gardening forever, housework whenever." I have no qualms about forgetting the dust indoors and concentrating on getting as much pleasure and benefit from being outdoors.

This is also the month when, circumstances permitting, I like to have a garden party. I usually choose a charity to support and then issue invites to as many people as possible to join me for morning coffee, lunch, or afternoon tea. I really enjoy the preparation for this: baking biscuits and savouries weeks in advance, filling the freezer, and then on the day, getting friends to help. I just enjoy serving lovely food and seeing people enjoy my garden.

This is also the time when I can spend long hours in my summerhouse, indulging in my love of crafts.

Quotes of the Month

All that is necessary for the triumph of evil is for good men to do nothing.
—Edmund Burke

God doesn't expect us to do great things, but to do small things with great love.
—Mother Theresa

Poem of the Month

<u>Love Is ...</u>

Love is patient, even when milk is spilled for the third time in one day.

Love is kind and never says what we deserve to hear.

Love does not envy, when he sleeps and you're up all night with a sick child.

Love does not boast, even when you've lost five pounds and she hasn't.

Love is not proud but is willing to be the first to say, "I'm sorry."

Love is not rude but speaks to family members as courteously as to guests.

Love is not self-seeking, even if it is your turn to choose.

Love is not easily angered, even if he did forget your anniversary.

Love keeps no record of wrong and never says, "I told you so."

Love does not delight in evil but rejoices in the truth.

Love always protects the innocent until proven guilty.

Love always trusts and expects the best of others.

Love always hopes to reconcile differences.

Love perseveres in accepting family members as they are, not as you want them to be.

Love never fails to make a strong and loving family.

—Author unknown

What to Do in June

Try making jam; if you don't have fruit growing in your garden or allotment, then keep a lookout in the shops for reasonably priced fruit that you could make jam from.

Many people grow fruit and veg, and they are usually quite willing to share if they have a glut. In my store cupboard, I usually have a supply of rhubarb jam, strawberry jam, raspberry jam, plum jam, and so on. The plums are from my own garden; I just have the one tree but can usually make loads of jam from it. I love jam on bread, I love to bake with it, and if the jam hasn't set very well (usually strawberry), I simply call it compote and stir it into rice puddings or yoghurt, or drizzle it over ice cream.

Fathers' Day also falls in June, so take the time to treat your dad.

Midsummer Day is also this month, another great excuse for a celebration. Why not have an outdoor party, invite family and friends, trim the garden with bunting and fairy lights? With lots of easy to prepare food, celebrate summertime in style.

My Garden in June

I am not a lover of growing vegetables, but I do have a herb garden. If you have a greenhouse (or even a large enough windowsill), try growing mixed salad leaves, garden rocket (arugula), cress, and so on. These are lovely to simply snip off what you need for a salad; you can plant at intervals to make sure of a continuous supply.

A favourite gardening job for me at this time of year is deadheading; the more you deadhead, the more flowers the plants will produce. Support any tall plants with canes or other supports. Hoe the borders continually; this is another of my favourite tasks, I could spend hours just hoeing the lovely brown earth, and it's a job which requires no bending.

When out walking my dog, I love to view other people's gardens and spot any plants I don't have but might like for the following year. It's also a good time to plant autumn flowering bulbs in any spare spots or tubs.

Money-Saving Tips

Saving money and avoiding waste is really important to me. We are able to buy a huge variety of sauces, pestos, pizza toppings, and so on from our supermarkets, but these can often lead to wasted leftovers, packages and bottles which have to be recycled. I now make as many sauces, salad dressings, and toppings as I can, many of which can be frozen in large or individual portions.

When I have a glut of milk in my fridge, I make parsley sauce or cheese sauce. A glut of tomatoes can provide sauces for bolognese, pasta, or pizza topping. Pesto can also be made from basil leaves, and spinach or kale will also work. Some recipes are included here, but just be inventive; use leftovers and create your own recipes.

Recipes of the Month

Basic White Sauce

This is the easiest and most foolproof way to make a sauce without lumps. Put 2 tablespoons plain flour in a medium saucepan, and slowly blend in 1 pint of milk; start by adding little by little until the whole pint is in. Then add 2 oz butter, and season with salt and pepper. Place on the stove, and slowly bring to the boil, stirring continuously. When bubbling, reduce the heat and stir for another few minutes to cook out the flour. Remove from the heat; if making cheese sauce, add your grated cheese (quantity is up to you; I add quite a lot, as I like it really cheesy). For parsley sauce, add a good handful of fresh chopped parsley; if using dried parsley, add to the pan when cooking. These sauces are lovely to use on cauliflower, broccoli, or any other veg of your choice. Store the sauce in small containers to freeze and use later.

Pesto Sauce

Ingredients
1½ oz pine nuts (or walnuts), 1½ oz cheese of your choice, ¼ pint virgin olive oil, 2 garlic cloves chopped fine, large bunch of basil leaves (or baby spinach or curly kale)

Method
Blend everything together, and keep in a glass jar in the fridge; shake well before using. Good with pasta or spread on top of fish before baking.

Mustard Salad Dressing

Ingredients
1 teaspoon Dijon mustard, 2 teaspoons whole-grain mustard (my preference is 3 teaspoons of Dijon mustard), 1 tablespoon cider vinegar, 3 tablespoons olive oil

Method
Mix the vinegar and mustards well. Slowly add the olive oil, whisking continuously until all is combined. Season according to taste with salt and pepper.

Keep in a jar in the fridge, shaking well before use.

Pasta Sauce

Ingredients

1 large onion, red or white, 1 or 2 cloves garlic (depending on taste), 1 lb fresh tomatoes or 1 large and 1 small tin chopped tomatoes, 1 red pepper or sweet pepper (not necessary if you don't have them), salt, pepper, and sugar. Any number of herbs can be added for flavouring, basil works really well, marjoram or oregano. Mushrooms, finely chopped can also be used, as always I use whatever I have to hand so flexibility is the key to this sauce.

Method

In a medium pan, add 1 tablespoon of olive oil, add chopped onion and cook until soft and just beginning to caramelise; add chopped garlic. (If using mushrooms or herbs add them at this point) Stir in chopped tomatoes (no need to skin, but you can if you prefer) and peppers, if using. Season with salt and pepper and 1 dessertspoon of sugar, bring to a simmer, and cook for about 1 hour, stirring occasionally. When cooled, pour into a blender to blitz.

I don't thicken this sauce, but if you wanted a stiffer consistency for pizza topping, you could add a tablespoon of flour or cornflour at the beginning, after the onion and garlic but before adding the tomatoes. I am never too specific about quantities; I just tend to use whatever I have. It may be less, or it maybe more. Again, this freezes really well and I use as a sauce for bolognese, adding to pasta, pizza topping, and so on.

Note: When cooking with tomatoes, always add some sugar to counteract any bitterness.

Mayonnaise

Ingredients

1 egg, 1 rounded teaspoon salt, 1 level teaspoon sugar, ½ level teaspoon dry mustard powder, ¼ level teaspoon freshly ground black pepper, 2 tablespoons white wine vinegar, ½ pint cold pressed rapeseed oil

Method

Place the egg and seasoning into a liquidizer, and mix until egg is frothy. Add vinegar, and mix again. Pour in oil very slowly whilst machine is running, until everything is well mixed.

Store in a glass jar in the fridge.

Ice Cream

When my children were small, I wanted to try making ice cream but, unfortunately, all the recipes I could find seemed to contain raw eggs. Not wanting to feed them raw eggs, I gave up on the idea.

However, in more recent times, I discovered recipes that thankfully didn't use eggs at all. So I began to experiment. The first recipe I tried was in a magazine and had quite a few ingredients, including 6 lemons. I made this recipe and duly froze the ice cream, but unfortunately, it was so hard, it was impossible to scoop it out of the box; very disappointing. So I experimented and eventually pared it down to just a few ingredients; the result was wonderful, creamy ice cream, so here is my version of this recipe:

Ingredients

1 large can condensed milk (405g), 10oz carton of double cream, fresh fruit of your choice

Method

Whip the double cream until thick, add the condensed milk. Fold in any fresh fruit of your choice (e.g., chopped strawberries, raspberries, or blueberries which are my favourite). Place mixture in a plastic container and freeze. I preferred this consistency; it is nice and easy to scoop, and you can try all sorts of variations.

Sometimes when I make this, I add a couple of tablespoons of cordial to the mixture; my favourites are ginger or elderflower cordial. I've also stirred through a small jar of salted caramel sauce or chocolate sauce. It's lovely to play around and add whatever you fancy.

Another version I experimented with was to add a dash of amaretto liqueur and some crumbled amaretto biscuits: divine.

Another easy recipe simply uses a carton of Greek yogurt; add 1 tablespoon good quality honey and 4 oz fresh or frozen berries. Blend everything together until smooth, place in container, and freeze until set.

Easy Summer Desserts

I love easy desserts for summer; these can be made individually and are perfect for outdoor eating and entertaining. Here are a few of my favourites:

Traditional Trifle

I make this in individual serving dishes. Place a trifle sponge, split and spread with jam, in the bottom of each dish. If wanted, add a dessertspoon of sherry. A layer of fruit is optional, but I like a fruit layer. Cover with custard, and after cooling, cover with double cream, and decorate with chocolate strands.

Minty Pots

On a visit to a stately home a couple of years ago, I bought a chocolate mint plant from the garden shop. Rubbing the leaves produced a lovely subtle chocolate smell, so I was determined to make something using this mint.

Ingredients

Handful of mint (or chocolate mint), 1 tub mascarpone, 150g pot natural yogurt, 2oz caster sugar, 1-2 drops green food colouring, zest of 1 lemon, 3 tablespoons lemon juice, 120ml double cream. For the chocolate sauce, 4oz dark chocolate, small carton double cream, 2 tablespoons caster sugar (or use 1 jar of ready-made chocolate sauce)

Method

Finely chop the mint leaves (saving a few for decoration) and blend with the mascarpone, yogurt, sugar, food colouring, lemon zest, and juice until smooth and creamy. Whip the cream until stiff, and fold into this mixture. Divide mixture between individual glasses and chill. Make chocolate sauce by melting chocolate with the cream and sugar until combined, leave to cool and pour over each glass; decorate with a couple of the reserved mint leaves.

Creamy Lemon Pots

A must for those who love lemons.

Ingredients

600 ml carton of double cream, 8oz caster sugar, 2oz lemon curd, 150 ml of fresh lemon juice, fresh fruit to decorate.

Method

Heat the cream, sugar, and lemon curd on a low heat, and bring to boiling point (boiling point has to be reached to make sure mixture will set). Simmer for 1 minute. Remove pan from heat and stir in the lemon juice. Chill until softly set, top with soft fruit of your choice (e.g., raspberries, strawberries, or blueberries).

A good quality sponge finger biscuit goes well with this dessert.

<u>Orange and Raisin Loaf</u>

Ingredients

6oz self-raising flour, 6oz caster sugar, 4oz margarine, 2 eggs, grated rind and juice of 1 orange, 4oz raisins

Method

Sift the flour and sugar in a bowl; add the margarine, eggs, orange juice, and zest; beat with a wooden spoon until smooth, and then add the raisins. Pour into a greased and lined loaf tin, and bake at gas mark 4 or 160 fan for about 55 minutes, until a skewer comes out clean. Leave to cool. When cold, decorate with icing sugar mixed with hot water, and decorate with orange candied slices.

July

What I Love about July

As the saying goes, "Hope springs eternal," and whereas July was once considered the height of summer, in these days of climate change with regard to our weather, we have learned to expect anything. Nevertheless, for me, the hope remains of long summer days, gardening, outings, holidays, picnics, and entertaining outdoors: a welcome change of routine for many.

Love it or hate it, this is the month when school is out. For about six to eight weeks, our children and grandchildren will be on holiday from school; when my children were school age, I absolutely loved the holidays. We spent the days on occasional outings, visiting grandparents, or simply relaxing at home and in the garden. It was so lovely to acquire grandchildren, which meant I could look forward to seeing much more of them. Always in my garden there would be lots to entertain, such as giant Jenga, giant tiddlywinks, hoopla, giant dominoes, and swing ball, to name a few.

Even as they grew older and more sophisticated, my grandchildren would still find fun in bubbles, giant sticks of chalk, and the old-fashioned bean bag. I, for one, think bean bags are entirely underrated. Being an avid gardener, football was always banned, so the bean bags were a great alternative for lobbing around the garden but causing minimal damage. They are great too for indoors, teaching small children how to throw and catch. They maybe old-fashioned, but I can still produce a bagful at the drop of hat, should they ever be required.

Quote of the Month

The way to gain a good reputation is to endeavour to be what you desire to appear.
—Socrates

Poem of the Month

Grandparents

Story Tellers

Meal Makers

Game Players

Loving lovers

Hugging huggers

Caring Carers.

—April Wright

The Dash, by Linda Ellis, is a brilliant poem which I love, but I couldn't get copyright permission to use it here. However, it is online, and you can read it there if you wish.

<u>What Is Wealth?</u>

Even though the treasures of our life are measured in men's terms of what is wealth,

Nothing that we shape from toil and strife compares to nature's bounty or to health

Men strive hard to build palaces for kings, calling on their talents and their skill,

Using precious stones and lovely things, paintings now adorn and objects fill!

But not a single object man can make, begins to match the natural display,

Surrounding every man who can partake, in nature's beauty all along the way.

The crystal that makes up a grain of sand, the feather as it floats upon the air.

The sea shell as it swirls into your hand, the water as it trickles without care.

The softness of the puppy's shiny fur, the hardness of the mossy jagged rock,

The rustle of the leaves as breeze makes stir, the sharpness of the crowing of the cock.

These gifts belong to all who have been blessed, with life by God, who is the fount of all,

And showers us with things that stand the test, for us to love until we hear the call.

—Dave Curtis (2004)

What to Do in July

No major indoor jobs for me in July, other than keeping the house in a reasonable order. If you spend the holiday away, lovely; if not, then spend as much time as possible outdoors, walking, gardening, eating outdoors or simply relaxing with a good book or newspaper. Time to catch up with friends and family. Take advantage of your local parks or beauty spots. When the sun is out, this is the best time to absorb that very necessary vitamin D.

Visiting a "pick your own" venue is always on my list of things to do; picking fruit in season for jams, baking, or just for eating is a lovely way to spend a day.

Strawberries are a lovely sign that the traditional cream tea can now be enjoyed. Host an afternoon cream tea in your garden, or treat yourself to visit the many places offering sumptuous cream teas.

My Garden in July

For me, the garden is my happy place, just as the kitchen is my happy place come the winter months, and I spend as much time as I can outdoors. I am either busy with gardening tasks, eating meals, or just relaxing with a cuppa and the newspaper or a good book, whilst sitting under my lovely shady gazebo.

Hoeing the borders is a favourite job. I never cover the soil with chippings or bark; I just love to see freshly hoed brown earth, and the robins always follow you around when you turn the earth.

Another essential job this month is to keep deadheading as much as possible; the more you deadhead, the more flowers will follow. My rose bushes always get a second feed to prolong the flowering season. When deadheading roses, don't just take off the flower head; go down the stem to a pair of leaves, this will keep the bush tidy.

Spring flowering bushes and plants can be pruned and shaped: lilac, bride of May, flowering currant, and so on. I am always on the lookout for cuttings from my plants and bushes, so before you discard, see if there are cuttings to be taken. It's so easy to take cuttings; trim to a few inches, cutting below leaf buds, and insert in a pot of compost. Keep in the greenhouse, and if successful, they are great to give to gardening friends as gifts or to sell as a fundraiser.

If you are lucky enough to have a wisteria, now is the time to prune. Cut back this season's growth, apart from shoots you wish to keep to train along supports. Tie in any straggling shoots to keep tidy, and then you prune again in January or February.

Wisteria flowers

Recipe of the Month

Many of my recipes in the summer are geared for easy entertaining and eating outdoors. I tend to focus on salads, quiches, and pates, all of which can be made in advance, in as large a quantity as you wish, saving you time in the kitchen.

Pea and Bean Salad

Many of my recipes are very ad hoc; I change them to suit whatever I have to hand. This pea and bean salad is very versatile, and it's lovely to have a large bowlful in the fridge. Use whatever you have, or change to add your own favourite ingredients. Here is what I use:

Ingredients

1 tin chickpeas, ½ tin spelt, ¼ tin aduki beans, quantity of frozen peas, red or green peppers, balsamic vinegar, lemon juice, 2 teaspoons mint sauce, a splash of rapeseed oil, and seasoning to taste

Method

Just mix everything together in a large bowl until you get a good consistency; keeps well in the fridge.

Sausagemeat Loaf

Another brilliant, versatile, and easy summer dish. It's great cold with salad or also served hot with new potatoes and veggies; it freezes very well.

Ingredients

1 lb pork sausage meat, large packet of stuffing of choice, 4 eggs, bacon, salt, and pepper

Method

Grease a 2lb loaf tin, and line bottom with bacon rashers. Make up stuffing mix and add to sausage meat, season well, and add 4 beaten eggs. Mix thoroughly, and place in tin, cover top with further bacon rashers, and bake for about 1 hour in a medium to hot oven. I find it best to turn this out whilst still warm.

Here are two very easy and generous recipes which are perfect for camping, picnics, or outdoor entertaining:

Campers' Fruit Cake

Ingredients

4oz margarine, 6oz sugar, 3 eggs, 6oz self-raising flour, 4oz sultanas, 4oz cherries, 4oz raisins, 1 teaspoon almond essence

Method

Cream together the margarine and sugar. Add the beaten eggs gradually, fold in the flour and then the dried fruit; cherries can be halved before adding. Lastly, add the almond essence. Spread into a greased and lined oblong tin, and bake at gas mark 4 or 160 fan for about 45 minutes, until golden and springy to the touch. When cooled, cut into squares.

Matilda Cake

Ingredients

6oz butter or margarine, 4oz sugar, 4oz chopped cherries, 10oz self-raising flour, 4oz sultanas, 2 dessertspoons golden syrup

Method

In a large saucepan, melt the margarine or butter with the sugar and syrup. Add all the remaining ingredients, mixing thoroughly. Pour into a large oblong greased and lined tin, and bake at gas mark 4 or fan 160 until golden brown. Cool and cut into squares.

August

What I Love about August

Total freedom! Normally I have quite a busy schedule as I belong to several groups which meet on either a weekly or monthly basis. But come August, everything ceases, so I have a whole month to contemplate how to spend my days free from all commitments and restrictions.

No one month can be designated as a holiday month, but when I was a child, July and August were when everyone took their annual holiday (this was known as the "works week"). Nowadays, it is more customary for people to take several holidays, spread over the year. My family were never great holiday takers, this stems from having two toddlers who both suffered from travel sickness and one large Labrador who also couldn't tolerate long journeys. Once, we had only travelled a few hundred yards when one toddler got sick, the dog weed all over the car, and we had to take the first of many emergency stops.

Another year, I loaded the pushchair with baby and toddler, and with the dog on his lead, we walked the last two miles into Skegness. This, coupled with the fact that we once lived in Norfolk with the beach and sea on our doorstep, sort of put us off booking holidays abroad. I always describe my holiday destinations as being either east or west coast (of Britain, that is).

Sometimes, we rush to other places for our entertainment, forgetting what we have on our doorstep. I recently bought a book with the title *111 Places in Sheffield That You Shouldn't Miss*. I took up this challenge and intended to visit each and every one, but my plan was thwarted by the COVID lockdown restrictions. However, as I write this, the whole nation is hoping things will soon get back to what we consider normal, and I will once again take up my explorations in and around Sheffield.

Quotes of the Month

Our children are being raised by appliances.
—Bill Moyers

Adversity has the effect of eliciting talents which, in prosperous circumstances, would have lain dormant.
—Horace

Poem of the Month

The Future

Even when the future seems enveloped in a cloud,

And knowing where to go your thoughts begin to crowd,

Your mind with many strange imaginings

Just stop and listen quietly to the wee small voice inside,

And write down what you hear, so thoughts and memories survive,

To be a guiding light to your next life initiative,

Step out in faith, so you may learn to live, to love and give.

Whatever God has planned for you to know, to be and do,

It isn't yours to question, but simply find the cue,

For your turn to walk on the stage of this almighty play,

And seek to give your best performance there upon your day,

A show that isn't about you, or anything you've done,

But all about obedience, and listening to the "One"

To whom we owe our everything, our life, our hope, our love!

Dave Curtis (2004)

What to Do in August

If you have children, the choice is probably not yours alone. Children will have their own ideas of things they wish to do and may need some direction as to what is actually feasible or affordable.

As a child, I can clearly remember not going anywhere during the long summer holiday, other than the local Working Men's Club outing for children. This was an event of great excitement for me and my sister; we were up early and packed off to the coach, where we were given a packet of crisps, a bottle of pop, and eight shillings to spend. The destination was usually Cleethorpes. For the rest of the holiday, we mostly spent time outdoors with other children, playing games of skipping, rounders, hide-and-seek, and so on, or visiting the local parks. What would our children of today make of this for a summer holiday? Whilst it is lovely to go on outings with our children or grandchildren we need to remember not to overdo the "entertainment", but to give our children time to be inventive and use their own imaginations.

If you aren't in charge of any children, then you are free to please yourself, with visits to older relatives, lunches out with friends, day trips, and so on; the list is endless. It's a good time to relax, take stock, and reflect on our lives, goals, and ambitions.

Jam making is so easy during August, with the plentiful supply of soft fruits. I love to see my store cupboard brimming with jars of delicious jams.

August in My Garden

I've never had much success with growing vegetables, but herbs are a great favourite in my garden. I have all the usual: parsley, sage, thyme, rosemary, bay tree, mint, and oregano. It's so lovely to pop outside to snip various herbs when cooking.

August is a time to give the herb patch some attention; herbs such as sage, marjoram, thyme, and tarragon will by now have become rather leggy. Give them a new lease of life by trimming well back and removing flowering stems.

Hydrangeas: This month is a good time to take cuttings from your plants; snip some nonflowering shoots, cutting below a pair of leaves. Prepare a few plant pots filled with compost and some grit sand, make a snip below the lowest leaf joint, and place in pot. When roots have developed, place individually in larger pots and keep watered. These make lovely gifts.

Lavender: This is one of my most favourite plants in my garden; I just love the combination of roses, lavender, and pinks. They form the biggest part in my long herbaceous border. When in flower, cut some stems for drying, making lavender bags or filling a bowl for a room fragrance. After flowering, cut the flowering stems right back, making a tidy shorter bush.

Plum tree: If you have a good crop of plums, make plum jam; this is one of the easiest jams to set. Some years, the tree gives lots of fruit; others, the harvest can be a bit sparse, in which case, just enjoy eating them. If you have birds or squirrels stealing your fruit, as I do, tie some unwanted CD discs to dangle around the branches; these are very good at deterring greedy wildlife.

Basket with hydrangea flowers and purple flowers

Lavender flowers in basket

Plums in baskets with vase of flowers

Jars of jam

Money-Saving Tips

Quite a lot of money can be saved when cooking meals by thinking ahead and making sure any leftovers are turned into further meals. It's surprising how many meals can be created from leftovers.

Vegetables: I always cook more vegetables than I need, and then any leftovers can be divided into foil trays and frozen, or covered with a cheese sauce. These make a really good instant meal to use with sausage or ham, or even just on their own. When boiling potatoes, do a few extra, and when cold, add some chopped chives and make a potato salad.

Lettuce: I used to really struggle with this, as I found it impossible to eat a whole head of lettuce before it turned that nasty, slimy green. However, after I tried a recipe a friend gave me for lettuce, pea, and mint soup, I now never waste lettuce.

Grated cheese: I never buy already grated cheese; not only is it more expensive, but something is added to make the cheese stay separate. Instead, I use a block of cheese and grate the whole thing; I always have a supply for jacket potatoes, cheese sauce, or salads.

Recipes of the Month

<u>Pea, Mint, and Lettuce soup</u>

Ingredients

1 large onion, 1 garlic clove chopped, 2 large white potatoes, 2 organic vegetable stock cubes, 8oz frozen peas, 1 large lettuce, fresh mint leaves chopped or 3 teaspoons of ready made mint sauce. Salt and pepper.

Method

Sauté 1 large onion until softened in butter or olive oil, add garlic.

Add 2 large potatoes, peeled and diced, together with 1½ pints of liquid, using 2 organic vegetable stock cubes.

Simmer until potatoes are cooked, and then add 8 oz frozen peas; cook for a further 5 minutes.

Lastly, add 1 chopped head of lettuce and 1 large handful of fresh chopped mint.

Cook until lettuce has wilted down, then season with salt and pepper, and liquidise.

This again is a versatile recipe; instead of lettuce, you could use any other salad leaf: lamb's lettuce, watercress, baby spinach, and so on.

I have never tried this soup chilled but bet it would be good on a hot summer's day.

Coconut and Lime Cake

A few years ago, when a friend's daughter was about to be married, I was asked to make a cake for the reception. It was a lovely idea, and a recipe card for the cake was placed on each table. I love this recipe, as it is one I made up myself.

Ingredients

For the cake: 8oz self-raising flour, 2oz coconut, 6oz margarine, 6oz caster sugar, 3 large eggs, 2 tablespoons lime marmalade, juice of 2 limes

For the icing: icing sugar, juice of 2 limes, toasted coconut

Before using the limes, grate all four and reserve the zest to use later for decoration.

Method

Warm the marmalade over a pan of hot water, add the juice of 2 limes, and combine well.

Cream the margarine and sugar, then gradually beat in the eggs.

Add marmalade mixture with a tablespoon of the flour, combine well. Add rest of flour and coconut.

Bake in either a greased and lined Swiss roll tin or 2 sandwich tins, whichever you prefer. Bake in a moderate oven, about 160/170 deg or gas mark 4-5, until golden brown.

Icing: mix icing sugar (I don't have a measurement for this; I just put a decent quantity in a bowl, probably about 8oz), mix with juice of a further 2 limes and hot water, if required, to get a thick coating consistency. Spread over the cake and decorate with the zest of the 4 limes and some toasted coconut.

Note: if toasting coconut, keep a close watch, as it browns very quickly and will easily burn.

If making a sandwich cake, I sandwich together with lime marmalade and a layer of soft icing, then decorate as before.

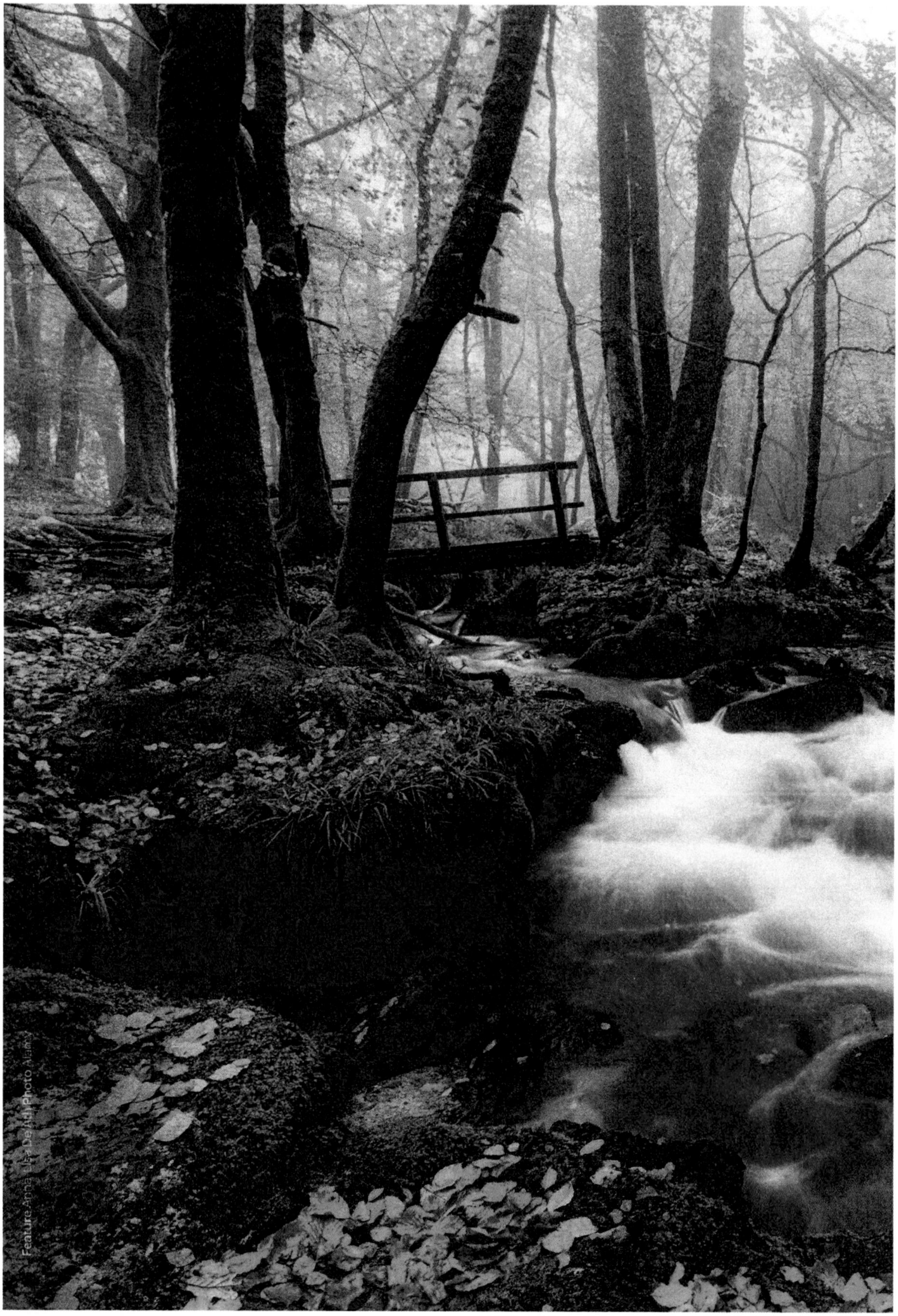

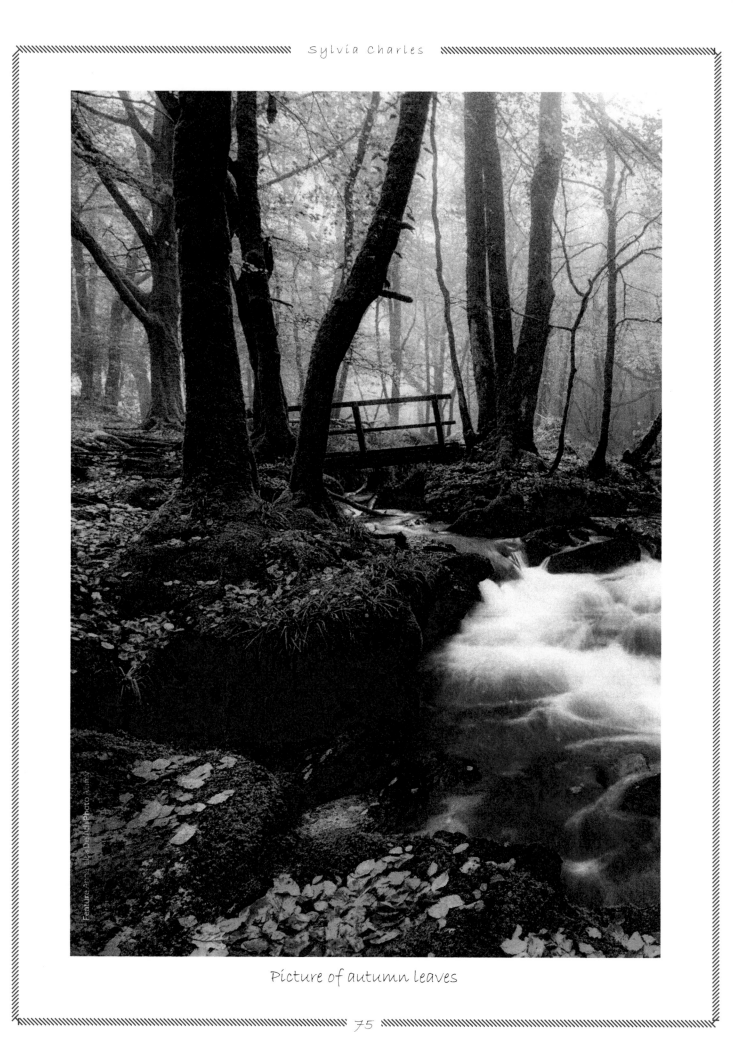

Picture of autumn leaves

September

What I Love about September

This is my very favourite month out of the whole year; I don't know why, but I absolutely look forward to September and enjoy it immensely. I am of the opinion that if all calendars were to disappear, I could always tell September by its smell. Damp, sometimes misty mornings, leaves starting with the first tinges of autumn colour, and for me, an unexplainable excitement hanging in the air. When I think of May (my other favourite month), it's all about promise; I do feel September is about reassurance. Nature has done its best to give an evocative, colourful display of all its bounty, but autumn seems to say it's all going away, but I'll take care of it until next spring, and the whole cycle will begin once more.

It is also the time when I begin to think about Christmas, but more of that later.

Quote of the Month

What we anticipate seldom occurs; what we least expect generally happens.
—Benjamin Disraeli

Poem of the Month

The following poem came about because Jennie, my daughter, grew tired of hearing me and my sister say, at the last panic-stricken minute of our neglected shopping and preparations, "Next year, we'll get organised early." Together with the poem came a little notebook covering September to December, with tips on what to do each week. I have to say I don't follow the ideas and tips rigorously, but I have found it most helpful, and it certainly does help me to be more organised and less stressed, so I will be sharing some of Jennie's tips and hints from now on until December.

For those people who think this is a little too early to be starting Christmas preparations, let me explain: As I am a Christian, getting the preparations out of the way early means that come December, the beginning of the Advent season, I can truly commit to pondering on the celebration of the coming of Jesus, as a baby, to save us all. So, hopefully, having done all the shopping and planning, I can really enjoy the Advent season.

Here's just a little present, that's sent from me to you

To make sure that your Christmas, runs smoothly and on cue.

There's no more need to panic, get frazzled, palpitate,

The only "cry" now should be, "Sylvia, check your date!"

It's all quite self-explaining, a page each week you flip,

From now on I am certain, through Christmas you will zip!

For really, most important, at this one time of year,

Is not to get caught up in commercial pomp and cheer.

These tasks all have their places, but that's where they should stay,

The price for over-stating, is one too dear to pay.

Oh, what opportunity, to celebrate true-worth,

God gave the bestest present, when Jesus came to earth ☺

—Jennie Wright

What to Do in September

Think about any extra big cleaning jobs around the house you want to complete. I call this time my Christmas clean, as opposed to the earlier spring clean. So basically I aim to do a thorough, all-through clean a couple of times a year.

Piccalilli, chutney, and mincemeat: September is the month I make pickles and chutneys, as they usually take around three months to mature and so are ready just in time for Christmas.

I make plenty, as jars of these make lovely Christmas gifts; people really enjoy food gifts, and I sometimes give a jar of piccalilli or chutney with a box of cheese biscuits and some speciality cheeses: a perfect gift. Home-made mincemeat is always lovely; it's easy to make and tastes so much better than shop-bought varieties.

The pantry also gets a good clear-out. I try and use up anything which is getting near (or past) its sell-by date and has been hidden at the back of the shelf. If you are a baker, find which cake recipe you will be using this year and make sure you have all the necessary ingredients or buy them early. Some supermarkets tend to run out of Christmassy goods near the end of December.

My daughter, Jennie, and I start shopping for what we call prizes for party games at Christmas. As a family, we love our party games, and it's lovely to have a bag of assorted prizes; who doesn't like a prize? We started out looking for little gifts, no more than 50p, but as the years went by, this became a pound, but by looking out for bargains of any sort, you can soon build up a decent stash of prizes. It's amazing how excited people can become over the most mundane items: dishcloths, combs, soap, sweets. The list is endless. Our favourite family games are charades, Scrabble, and Pictionary, but the game we love most is what we call the Card Game. I'll include how to play this; we also play it at group Christmas parties as well as at home. It is really popular, and the children especially love it.

Our NanNan's Card Game

We always call this NanNan's Card Game, as it was something she used to play at her dance group socials; after she gave us the instructions, we played it every Christmas and continue to do so. It's a lovely reminder of her.

You will need 2 packs of playing cards.

Bag of assorted prizes

Small table to display prizes (depending on how many are playing, put plenty of prizes as they can sometimes run out before the game is ended)

Divide one pack of playing cards evenly between all players (if they can't be divided equally put the spare cards to one side).

One person needs to be the caller with the other pack (it is possible to be the caller and still take part in the game).

The caller calls out the first card in their pack; whoever has the identical card places their card face down and selects a prize. This prize must be on display, as someone else could claim that prize.

The game continues with the caller calling each card; whoever has the same card can either chose a prize from the centre or claim a prize that someone else has already won (this causes much rivalry, and usually there is one or two prizes which prove the most sought after).

When a player uses all their cards, they can claim and keep all the prizes in their possession. These are no longer part of the game.

My Garden in September

I keep my borders tidy by cutting back any flowering plants which have definitely finished. I remove all faded flower heads but allow the leaves to die back naturally; this means the leaves will feed the bulbs and roots for next year. However, if you wish to gather seeds, leave a few flower heads until they are dry. Collect and save these in paper bags in a dry place, ready to plant in trays come spring. (It's helpful to label the bags with the name of the plants)

About this time, I stop feeding summer flowering plants and shrubs in containers, but start to feed any winter flowering shrubs (e.g., rhododendrons and winter flowering clematis). I feed these monthly to begin with but more regularly once they start flowering.

Buy winter flowering bulbs for borders and containers; planting usually begins next month, but it's nice to get them early and start planning your planting.

Indoor cyclamen which have been dormant over the summer months can now be cleaned up, repotted, and brought indoors; start to water gradually.

Make sure any plant pots you are storing are washed and clean; dirty plant pots can spread disease, especially in the greenhouse.

Recipes of the Month

<u>Lemon Meringue Pie</u>

This is another family favourite; I've made this for years. It's not as difficult as you might imagine, so if you haven't made one before, give it a try.

Ingredients

Biscuit base: 5oz digestive biscuits, 3oz butter or margarine

Filling: 1½oz cornflour, 3oz light brown sugar, ½ pint water, rind and juice of 2 lemons, 1oz butter, 2 egg yolks

Meringue: 2 egg whites, 4oz castor sugar

Method

Melt the butter, and add the crushed digestive biscuits. Mix well, and spread in a greased pie dish. Leave to chill.

In a saucepan, mix the cornflour with the water; add sugar, lemon rind, and juice; bring slowly to the boil, stirring all the time. Simmer for 2-3 minutes until thickened, then remove from heat, add the butter and egg yolks. Mix well, and pour gently onto biscuit base.

Beat the 2 egg whites until stiff peaks form, add half the sugar and beat again until peaky, fold in remaining sugar, beat again, and pile on top of pie filling. Brown meringue in a hot oven.

A pastry case can also be used, but bake this blind first of all.

This is also extremely good made up as a rhubarb meringue; follow the same as the biscuit base, but add 1 teaspoon of ground ginger. If using fresh rhubarb, cut into smallish pieces and put in a saucepan with 1 tablespoon of water and 1 tablespoon of sugar. Cook for about 10 minutes until it forms a puree, mix 1 tablespoon of cornflour with a little water and add to the pan, cook until mixture thickens, and then add the 2 egg yolks. If I don't have any fresh rhubarb, then I just use a jar of rhubarb and ginger jam. Lovely.

Ginger Biscuits

My recipe folder has several versions of ginger biscuits, but this one is my favourite:

Ingredients

10oz plain flour, 1 teaspoon baking powder, 2 teaspoons ground ginger, 1 teaspoon cinnamon, 5oz butter diced, 4oz castor or light brown sugar, 2 tablespoons golden syrup, 1 medium egg beaten

Method

Put the flour, baking powder, and spices into a mixing bowl.

Add butter and sugar, and rub in until mixture resembles breadcrumbs.

Mix in the syrup and egg to make a stiff dough, shape into a round, and refrigerate for about 1 hour to allow it to firm up enough to roll out.

Roll out dough, and cut into shapes. Place on baking trays lined with greaseproof or baking paper.

Bake for 10-15 minutes at gas mark 4 or 160 fan, until golden brown.

This makes a large quantity, so I usually cover some in melted chocolate, leaving others plain; they're lovely for dunking.

Also makes lovely gingerbread men.

October

What I Love about October

I love the amazing colours of leaves as they turn from shades of green to wonderful hues of brown, orange, and red. Some years we get wonderful weather in October, perfect for lovely long walks or maybe, in some years, still time to sit outdoors. As a keen (but very amateur) photographer; I love to take my camera and capture some of the inspiring trees and hedgerows as they slowly but surely start to turn into their autumnal glory. I also love taking photos of skyscapes, even from my back garden. I get wonderful sunsets. Once I have had my photographs developed I turn them into greeting cards.

It will be half-term for most children, and this is a lovely way to spend time enjoying family activities and outings.

Quotes of the Month

When was the last time you tried something new? Every
once in a while, try and do something new.

Never look down on anyone unless you're helping them up.

One small positive thought in the morning can change your whole day.

Before you speak, Think:

T = is it true?

H = is it helpful?

I = is it inspiring?

N = is it necessary?

K = is it kind?

All these quotes or sayings were given to me by my granddaughter April; thank you,
April, for these wise words.

Poem of the Month

I have a small collection of very old books, and as I was browsing through one, I came across the following poem, which completely enthralled me. The book is called *Home Words (for Heart and Hearth)*; it was printed in 1903.

The Battle of Life

Go forth in the battle of life my boy, go while it is called today;

For the years go out and the years come in, regardless of those who may lose or win, of those who may work or play.

There is room for you in the ranks, my boy, and duty, too, assigned,

Step into the front with a cheerful grace,

Be quick, or another may take your place, and you may be left behind.

There is work to do by the way, my boy, that you never can tread again;

Work for the loftiest, lowliness man – Work for the plough, adze, spindle and pen; work for the hands and the brain.

Yes, evil will follow your steps, my boy, to lay for your feet a snare;

And pleasure sits in her fairy bowers, with garlands of poppies and lotus flowers enwreathing her golden hair.

Then put on the armour of God, my boy, in the beautiful days of youth:

Put on the helmet, breast plate, and shield,

And the sword that the feeblest arm may wield, In the cause of right and truth.

And go to the battle of life, my boy, with the peace of the Gospel shod;

And "strong in the Lord" by "The Spirit's might";

Thou shalt conquer the foe in the holy fight,

And wear the crown of God."

—A Sower

What to Do in October

This is a great time to make your Christmas cake; by making it early, there will be plenty of time for the traditional soaking with brandy every three weeks or so. As it is half-term, let the children help with the weighing of the dried fruit and mixing it all together. Even though my children and grandchildren are no longer on hand, I still stick to the routine of making my cake at half-term.

Christmas cards: I check on what I may have left from last year and then try to make as many myself by upcycling last year's cards sent to me and donated by friends and family. If I have to buy, then I stick to buying the charity ones.

It's good to make a specific list of the gifts you are likely to buy; this saves impulse buying later in the year. Again, I try and factor in some handmade gifts and foodie hampers. In our family, we love receiving foodie gifts; make a list of which items you would include and buy, spreading the cost over the coming weeks.

My Garden in October

This is traditionally a time for planting daffodil bulbs; I make a note of where there have been blank spaces in my borders and fill them with spring and summer bulbs. I always indicate with canes where I have planted, as I am prone to dig them up. It's good to also fill a few pots with bulbs so you can move them around in spring, to ensure colour wherever you need it.

Any tidying jobs done now will save time come next spring; cut back dead growth on perennials, shape any bushes or trees, and give roses a half-prune to prevent wind rock on their roots.

Money-Saving Tips

Rather than letting the sage bushes in the herb bed go to waste, I have a couple of recipes for using quite a large quantity.

Sage and Onion Stuffing:

Chop 1 medium onion, and fry in 2 oz butter. Remove from heat, and stir in 3 oz white breadcrumbs, about a handful of chopped sage leaves, 1 large beaten egg, salt and pepper, and 4 tablespoons of milk. If using at once, transfer to a greased baking dish and bake for 20 minutes or so in a hot oven. If I am freezing this, I tend to freeze, uncooked, in small individual dishes or tartlet tins, ready to bake as required.

You can add whatever ingredients you fancy (e.g., chopped apple, cranberries, mushrooms, nuts).

Cheese, sage, and onion scones:

12oz onions chopped, olive oil, 12oz self-raising flour, 2 teaspoons salt, 2 teaspoons dry mustard powder, handful of chopped fresh sage leaves, 4oz grated cheese, 1 egg, milk to mix.

Cook the onions in olive oil until nice and soft. Combine the flour, salt, mustard powder, grated cheese, and sage in a mixing bowl, then add the onions and mix everything until well combined. Mix egg with milk and use enough to make a soft dough. Roll out and cut into large scones; bake until golden brown, gas mark 6 or 180 fan.

These are lovely with soup, served warm and buttered.

Having previously mentioned my weekly delivery of the Riverford organic veggie box, which has a weekly newsletter, I was so impressed with this copy, I wanted to share it. Hope you enjoy reading it.

GUY'S NEWS
No Time to Waste

Perhaps the worst thing about wasting food is the contempt it shows for the planet that produced it. An abiding memory of my father will be his 90-year-old bottom upended while skip-diving for waste veg for his supper. I was always trying to persuade him to take some of the fresh stuff, but his parsimonious pleasure in eating what others rejected grew with age. Some measure their success by what they control and consume; he was the opposite. His final, increasingly eccentric years set an example that I admire more as I age myself.

Most of us (Riverford customers at least) hate waste; some of us are willing to accept imperfection to avoid it, and a few even cherish the irregularity that nature lends to our food. Yet supermarkets are sterile, uniform places, and produce must match their strict specifications. Any cauli under 11cm, any courgette over 14cm, any Little Gem under 130g, any misshapen carrot or blemished potato, any sign of a slug, aphid or caterpillar; all are rendered worthless. Short-lived, headline-grabbing campaigns on wonky veg do little to drive a lasting reduction in waste.

Riverford does have specifications – but we invite growers to help us write them, to challenge them, and to ask for exemptions when a crop struggles to meet them. Our guidance is based on eating quality rather than cosmetics, and on you not having to spend ages trimming around bruised potatoes or carrot fly damage. I check what goes in the waste trailer, and challenge the team if I think they are being too harsh – but almost invariably they get the balance right. What isn't quite good enough for you is used in our canteen and restaurant, given to co-owners, donated to our charity partners FoodCycle and Food in Community, and lastly, fed to the cows – or the compost heap, if we are worried about alliums tainting the milk. Although there is virtually no 'waste', it is worth considering that waste in the field comes at a very low environmental cost, returned to the soil from whence it came. By the time it has been picked, graded, packed, stored and transported, its environmental impact has multiplied by about six, even before the impact of disposal; worst of all is cooking too much and scraping it into the bin.

Our new campaign, No Time to Waste, is on a mission to reduce food waste at home. We'll be sharing tips, recipes and more on all our channels, plus a weekly challenge, No Waste Wednesdays, on our Facebook group Riverford Hive. Join us.

Monday 1st March 2021   riverford.co.uk   01803 227227
Printed on 100% recycled paper

This newsletter was initially written for and distributed in the Riverford organic veg boxes. Founder Guy Singh-Watson writes a weekly newsletter in the veg boxes, which can also be read via Riverford's magazine, Wicked Leeks, by signing up at www.wickedleeks.riverford.co.uk/#join

Recipes of the Month

Soup It Up

A few years ago, I was asked to give a talk to a group of people who were interested in growing and cooking their own vegetables. I gave the talk the name "Soup It Up." I am an avid soup eater, having some variety of soup almost every day of the year. My weekly Riverford organic veggie box means I am never short of vegetables to experiment with. Hope you enjoy my tips and recipes:

Soup-Making Tips

- Always sauté vegetables in either oil or butter before adding liquid; this improves the flavour.
- Use organic vegetable stock cubes and lots of black pepper.
- No need to add salt; use herbs instead (dried or fresh).
- Most soups are blended, but the ones I don't blend are mushroom, chorizo, chickpea, and chunky vegetable soups.
- I freeze individual portions or keep in the fridge for 3-4 days; can be heated slowly straight from the freezer.
- For special occasions, serve with croutons and cream.
- Any combination works well, but I usually stick to colours (e.g., anything green together or yellow and orange together).
- Add onion, carrot, and celery to most varieties (except mushroom) for flavour.
- Red onions are preferable in carrot soup.
- No need to measure out ingredients.

Try out these various vegetable combinations:

- carrot, sweet potato, butternut squash, or any other squash
- potato and leek
- broccoli and courgette
- Spinach, can be added to any soup, but only add at the end for a few minutes to wilt.
- Watercress (same as spinach)
- Mushrooms
- Tomato, red peppers or sweet peppers
- Celeriac, parsnips, and swedes.
- Friday Soup: anything goes, colour irrelevant.

You can add broth mix or pasta to bulk a soup out

Basically, anything goes. It's all down to individual taste.

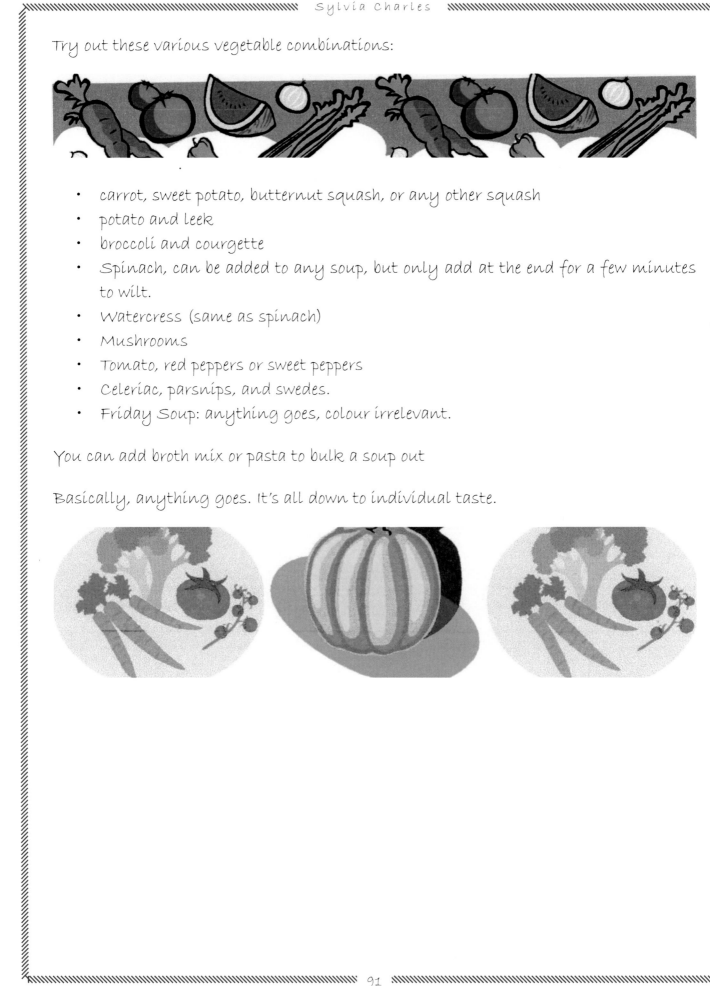

Carrot Soup

Ingredients

Butter or olive oil, 2lb carrots, 2 large onions, 2 cloves garlic, 2 organic vegetable cubes.

Method

Melt butter or oil in large pan. Add chopped onions to soften, add sliced carrots and cover with stock cubes dissolved in 2 pints hot water. Season with salt and pepper, bring up to the boil then simmer for 30 minutes. Cool then liquidise.

Celery Soup

Ingredients

Butter or olive oil, 1 head of celery, 1 large onion, 1 large potato, black pepper,1.1/2 pints boiling water, 2 organic vegetable stock cubes

Method

Melt butter or oil in large pan, add chopped vegetables and sauté for 10 minutes. Add stock cubes dissolved in boiling water. Season with black pepper. Bring to boil and simmer for 20 minutes; cool and blend.

Chick Pea and Chorizo Soup

Ingredients

Piece Chorizo sausage, 2 or 3 stalks of celery, 1 large onion, 2 cloves garlic, 1 tin chick peas, 2 tins chopped tomatoes, 1 litre of vegetable stock, (using 2 organic vegetable stock cubes), salt, pepper and 2 teaspoons sugar, 1 bag baby spinach.

Method

In a large saucepan, fry chopped sausage in a little olive oil for a few minutes.

Add chopped onion, celery, and garlic, and cook until celery softens. Add seasoning. Add chick peas (including liquid). Add tomatoes and sugar, together with vegetable stock.

Cook for 20 minutes, then add bag of washed baby spinach; cook for a further 5 minutes until spinach has wilted.

Broccoli, Bean, and Pasta Soup

Ingredients

2 tablespoons Olive Oil, 1 large onion, chopped, 3-4 garlic cloves, crushed, black pepper, ½ teaspoon dried oregano, 1 head of broccoli finely chopped (including stalk), 2 sprigs fresh thyme, 2 tins Haricot or Cannellini beans, drained, 1 litre vegetable stock, 100g small pasta shapes.

Method

Heat olive oil in large pan, add chopped onion, and cook gently until onion softens, then add garlic and herbs. Season with pepper, add broccoli, and cook for 5 minutes; next, stir in beans and stock, bring to boil. and simmer 15 minutes. Add pasta and simmer until pasta is cooked.

Curried Parsnip Soup

Ingredients

1½ lb parsnips, olive oil or butter, 2 chopped onions, 2 cloves garlic, 2 pints vegetable stock, 1 teaspoon coriander seeds, 1 teaspoon cumin seeds, (crushed if using seeds or you can use dried) 1 teaspoon turmeric, 1 teaspoon ginger, salt and pepper.

Method

Heat butter or oil and cook onion until   soft. Add garlic and cook a further 2 minutes.   Add all spices, turmeric, and ginger, and cook a few more minutes. Then add chopped parsnips, stir well, add stock, and season. Simmer the soup for about 1 hour, uncovered. Cool and then blend.

Mushroom Soup

Ingredients

1 oz butter, 1 oz plain flour, ½ pint chicken stock, plus ½ pint milk

1 tablespoon chopped fresh parsley (or ½ dessertspoon dried), approx. 4 oz mushrooms, wiped and chopped, black pepper, fresh cream (optional)

Method

Place all ingredients (except fresh cream) in a saucepan, and bring to the boil, stirring continuously.

Cover and simmer for 10-15 minutes.

Remove from heat and add cream (if using).

Enjoy.

I never blend this soup, as the mushrooms break down during cooking, but you can blend if you prefer a smoother version..

November

What I Love about November

Well, the first thing I love is that this is the month of my birthday. Some people would say that as they get older, they prefer to forget birthdays, but not me. One can never have too many birthdays (considering the alternative).

My home always has a numerous supply of snuggle rugs, and this is the month when I start to hunt them all out. Nothing is nicer than curling up wrapped in a fleecy rug to read, watch tele, or maybe have a nap!

Quote of the Month

We make a living by what we get, but we make a life by what we give.

Success is the ability to go from one failure to another with no loss of enthusiasm.
.   —Winston Churchill

Poems of the Month

Something seemed to whisper as he stood upon the sand

And watched the white capped waves come in and rest upon the sand

There's not a rock out yonder where the blue waters play

But has experienced more of life than the oldest man today

What is the process working? Why should the waters move?

What is it that sky and earth and stream and stars were meant to prove?

Any why is man so feeble and granite made so strong?

And why must pain be suffered if life is not for long?

There, by the blue lake standing, a great rock seemed to say,

Man still will come to question ten thousand years away

But all I've learned I'll tell you, it cannot be for nought,

That white waves breaking on a ledge can stir man's deepest thoughts.

—Unknown

Memories

Painting pictures in my mind, memories of life gone past,

Some are faint and hide behind, a misty screen, a hazy cast.

But all these things that I remember, living still inside my head,

Are precious gold, just like September, clinging leaves, they're not quite dead.

This precious store of life's reflections, grows much greater as we go,

No one else has our collection, we control our memory flow.

Written in our mind's great diary, all our life's encounters lie,

Some of them are hot and fiery, others tranquil, blue as sky.

People's faces, family, friends, clear as on the day they left,

Some are happy, others painful, years have passed, yet still bereft.

Isn't it a wonder though, that we can sit and care,

Of times, that even though they've passed, our memory holds them there?

—Dave Curtis (2004)

<u>Ordinary People</u>

Ordinary people there with ordinary faces,

Ordinary circumstance, in ordinary places.

Living life the way they have, through every generation,

Earning money, eating bread, forgetting their relation

To greater purpose in their life, than pleasure for their lover,

But missing something obvious, that they must yet discover,

That if they listen to "the Word," that's waiting down inside,

The messages, deep hidden there, have meaning quite worldwide.

The oneness of the human race, is really so astounding,

If we seek opportunities, we could bring understanding.

Our cultures and our history, and how we came to talking,

In blissful ignorance we live, instead of jointly walking,

Along a path that we discover, leads us on the way,

To comprehending greater things, than "who is right" today,

But seeking common good in all, we must make the decision,

To work together, asking God, to heal the world's division.

—Dave Curtis (2004)

What to Do in November

If you have made a Christmas cake, the flavour and moistness will deepen by feeding it with brandy every two to three weeks.

Spread the cost of postage stamps by buying a few each week.

Start to plan for the Christmas holiday (e.g., where will you be going, who will you be entertaining?). I love browsing through my Christmas cookery books and magazines to plan menus.

In mid-November, It's time to retrieve my Christmas decorations, as I like to start the trimming up on the 1st December, adding more each week until by Christmas, the house is fully decked out.

For Christmas shopping, I do as much gift buying as I can in November.

Towards the end of the month, check all outside lights; again, I like to have the outdoor lights all in place ready to switch on the 1st of December to herald the start of the Advent season.

It's lovely to make a candle arrangement, lighting one candle each week during Advent.

If you are a crafter, magazines are full of ideas for little gifts to knit, crochet, or fashion. I like to have a stash of these for extra stocking fillers.

My Garden in November

This is the month I gradually make a retreat from the garden, unless on a fine day I can manage a bit more tidying of the borders. This is also the month for planting tulip bulbs; plant them as deep as you can. Depending on the size and content of your garden, it may be possible to make your own Christmas wreath, evergreen leaves, ivy, anything with berries will make a lovely wreath. If you have any long strands of anything you have pruned (e.g., honeysuckle, wisteria, clematis), you can make your own wreath base; as a rule, if you can wrap something round your wrist without it breaking, you can make a circular wreath from it. Secure with string, which will be hidden once decorated.

Money-Saving Tips

This has to be the best time for trying to save money, as we all tend to overspend at Christmas.

Gifts: When buying for family and friends, it's a good idea to find out what they'd actually like to receive; it's such a waste of money to buy things which are not wanted, or needed, and may be discarded afterwards.

Set yourself a budget you know you can afford, and don't be tempted to exceed it. It's the thought behind a gift that matters, not how much it cost.

Wrapping paper: Although the wrapping paper to buy can be beautiful and desirable, an awful lot of it won't be recyclable. I use plain brown wrapping paper but am imaginative with ribbons, home-made gift tags, and so on to pretty up the parcel.

I have included my pattern for knitted Christmas puddings; these make brilliant table decorations, or make six of them and package in decorated egg boxes. These make a box of chocolates go a long way and are so inexpensive to make.

How to knit a Christmas Pudding, complete with Chocolate

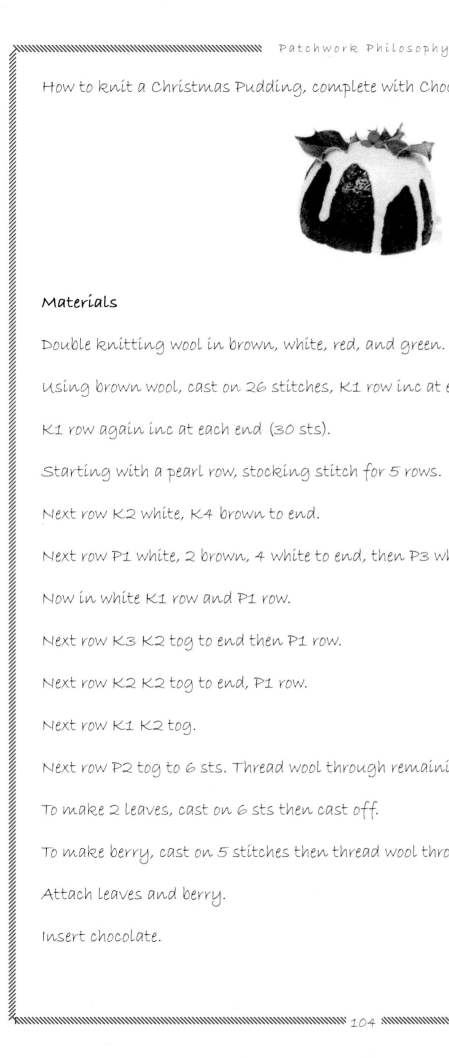

Materials

Double knitting wool in brown, white, red, and green. No. 11 knitting needles.

Using brown wool, cast on 26 stitches, K1 row inc at each end (28 sts).

K1 row again inc at each end (30 sts).

Starting with a pearl row, stocking stitch for 5 rows.

Next row K2 white, K4 brown to end.

Next row P1 white, 2 brown, 4 white to end, then P3 white.

Now in white K1 row and P1 row.

Next row K3 K2 tog to end then P1 row.

Next row K2 K2 tog to end, P1 row.

Next row K1 K2 tog.

Next row P2 tog to 6 sts. Thread wool through remaining sts and stitch up side.

To make 2 leaves, cast on 6 sts then cast off.

To make berry, cast on 5 stitches then thread wool through and tie off.

Attach leaves and berry.

Insert chocolate.

Recipes of the Month

<u>Lancashire Hot Pot</u>

Come this time of year, I am more than ready to start enjoying warming casseroles; for some reason, Lancashire Hot Pot was one I had not made for ages, but I recently found myself in the butcher's shop, admiring the lovely lamb chops, so thought it was about time to make this once more. I am not sure if it is the traditional Lancashire recipe, but it is the one I have always used since my children were small.

Ingredients

Lamb chops (allow 2 chops per person), onions, carrots, salt and pepper, potatoes, 2 organic lamb stock cubes

Method

Place lamb chops in large casserole dish.

Cover with layer of onions and carrots; chop the vegetables quite thickly, as it is in the oven for a long time. Season with salt and pepper.

Slice the potatoes quite thickly and arrange in overlapping layers on top of the dish. Cover with the stock cubes dissolved in enough water to almost come to the top, but don't cover the potatoes.

Place casserole in oven at a medium heat for about an hour or an hour and a half. Remove the lid, and cook for a further 30 minutes to allow potatoes to brown.

Serve with a green vegetable.

<u>Lamb Chop Soup</u>

Forgive me for including yet another soup recipe, but this is one I discovered by accident after making the hot pot recipe, and it was so delicious and tasty, I shall be making the hot pot more often, just so I can get this soup. After we finished the hot pot, I was left with a large quantity of the casserole (minus the lamb chops, of course). Not wanting to freeze the leftovers, I decided to liquidise the whole lot and call it soup. I couldn't believe how the flavour of lamb chops came through; it's definitely on my list of favourite soups now.

Fruit Gingerbread

Ingredients

4oz margarine, 4oz each of black treacle and golden syrup, ¼ pint milk, 2 eggs, 8oz plain flour, 2oz brown sugar, 1 tablespoon ground ginger, 1 teaspoon bicarbonate of soda, 4oz sultanas

Method

Melt the margarine, treacle, and syrup in a pan. Add the milk, and leave to cool. Add the beaten eggs.

Pour over the dry ingredients, and add the sultanas. Pour into a large greased and lined tray, and bake at gas mark 2 for about 40 minutes, until firm to the touch.

Keep for 2 days, wrapped in greaseproof before slicing.

This is the sort of recipe I love, as you can either treat it as a traybake or call it a pudding; delicious served warmed with some extra golden syrup drizzled over the top with hot custard or, if preferred, ice cream.

Christmas Pudding

I haven't included a recipe for Christmas pudding because as with Christmas cakes, magazines and newspapers will be full of tempting recipes for you to try. November is the traditional time for making a pudding on what is called "Stir Up Sunday."

I can only say that if you do make one, you will never again want to eat a shop-bought one. I make one in a 2 pint pudding basin, and the leftovers are mouth-wateringly delicious, warmed and served with brandy sauce, custard, or leftover brandy butter.

A winter scene

Winter

This picture, called *First Snow*, is a print made from an original watercolour painting by David Charles (my husband) Needless to say, he has given permission for this to be reproduced.

December

What I Love about December

In one word, Christmas. The preparations, the planning, the anticipation of family gatherings, and, for me as a Christian, the true celebration of God sending Jesus as a baby to save us all.

Quotes of the Month

It is possible to give without loving, but it is impossible to love without giving.
—Richard Braunstein

When God is about to do something great, He starts with a difficulty; When He is about to do something truly magnificent, He starts with an impossibility.
—Armin Gesswein

Men and women everywhere sigh on 26th December and say they're glad Christmas is all over for another year. But, it isn't over, "Unto you is born ... a Saviour"—it's just beginning! And it will go on forever.
—Eugenia Price

Poems of the Month

A Christmas Gift

Come buy! Come buy! Shop windows cry, come save on special offers,

Don't hesitate, you'll be too late, come fill our bursting coffers.

With shelves piled high to catch the eye, of every person passing,

A spending spree of Christmas glee, each trader is amassing.

I stand among the bustling throng and watch them hurry by me,

The glittering windows all around have Christmas gifts to ply me.

I look and sigh and wonder why the shops have all the glory,

While the churches empty of their flock, retell the Christmas story.

A tale of babe in manger laid and shepherds fast asleep,

Of Angel song they brought along, a lamb to Jesus' feet.

The story then tells of three men whose wisdom was renown,

They sought a King their gifts to bring and leave at Bethlehem town.

A simple tale, and almost pale against today's accounts,

And yet the giving is the same in large or small amounts.

That tale of fame applies the same today as years ago,

Shepherds and Kings gave precious things because they loved him so.

And surely we our friendship see as something worth a price,

What better way to show our love than giving something nice.

There is a time to give too much, a time to overspend,

That time is Christmas with a gift that says "I love you, friend."

—Terry Funnell (from his book, *Feelings*)

Just Another Tale?

Just two peering faces in the evening gloom,
Trying to find places, searching for a room.
Just a worried husband concerned to go no more,
Finding in a strange land no one at the door.
Just a friendly landlord at the local inn,
Giving all he could afford; a barn to shelter in.
Just a group of cattle watching in the night,
Hearing vessels rattle round a lantern light.
Just another labour, no one close at hand,
Nothing in her favour but a swaddling band.
Just a weary flock of sheep there to see the scene,
First to hear the baby weep in that stable mean.
Just another baby, another mouth to feed,
Born of mortal lady, yet of Godly seed.
Just a child and mother sheltering in a barn,
Just like any other, trying to keep warm.
Just a rough hewn manger where the baby laid,
A refugee, a stranger, was the price He paid.
Just another story? No; that babe is King,
And of His power and glory may we forever sing

—Terry Funnell (from his book, *Feelings*)

What to Do in December

After the last soaking of brandy, marzipan and decorate the cake.

Complete all decorations, inside and out

Make sure orders are in for turkey and other meats.

Post cards and parcels early.

Check out what's on at your local church. There are sure to be activities for the children, carol services, and so on.

Hope the tips for organising Christmas have been useful; the last entry in Jennie's notebook was "Smile ☺ and have a Happy Christmas."

The same to you all.

Money-Saving Tips

I've already mentioned ways to save on wrapping paper and cards, but what about those essential Christmas crackers? Boxes of shop-bought crackers look so appealing and attractive but are, oh so, expensive. Why not try making your own? It's easier than you think. For a traditional cracker shape, save cardboard tubes and wrap in fabric, crepe paper, or tissue paper, and decorate with ribbons, lace, small baubles, and so on. You can then personalise each one by inserting small gifts suitable for each recipient. An alternative way, if you don't fancy making the traditional shape, is to make small cardboard boxes; they can be filled with something of interest for each person and decorated with ribbon and a name tag.

Careful management of leftover food will save money on many meals after Christmas Day.

Recipes of the Month

Christmas Pie

I always make this version of a pork pie after Christmas to use up any leftover meat.

Line a cake tin with shortcrust pastry, saving enough for the pastry lid. A packet of shop-bought shortcrust pastry will do. Although I do prefer to make my own pastry, I have to admit to always having shop-bought shortcrust and puff pastry in my freezer for emergency. No one wants to spend time making pastry just after Christmas, so this is where readymade comes in very handy.

For the filling, I always use cooked meat (turkey, ham, sausages), stuffing, cheeses, or whatever you have left over. This is a multilayered pie, and I intersperse each layer of diced meat with stuffing, cheese, cranberry sauce, my Christmas chutney (which was made in September), or piccalilli. When you have layered all your leftovers, press down and cover with a pastry lid. Brush with beaten egg, and bake until pie is hot and golden.

This goes down extremely well with all my family and is a marvellous way of ensuring nothing gets wasted.

Mincemeat Bakewell

This is the Christmas version of my Bakewell tart.

Line a cake tin with shortcrust pastry, and spread with mincemeat.

For the topping, beat together 2oz margarine, 2oz sugar, 1 egg, 1oz ground almonds, 1oz self-raising flour, 1 teaspoon almond extract, and ½ teaspoon vanilla extract. Spread this over the mincemeat, and bake at gas mark 5 for 10 minutes, then turn oven down to gas mark 4 for about 20 minutes. When cooled, this can be left plain or iced and decorated with almond flakes. If left plain, it goes very well with any leftover brandy butter or cream.

Vegetable Pie

I always have loads of cooked vegetables left over, and fresh veggies can also be cooked and incorporated into this pie. My version is to fry one large onion, add some sliced mushrooms, then add all the cooked vegetables. Mix well, place in a dish, and cover with grated cheese of your choice. This can then be covered with breadcrumbs mixed with some fresh or dried herbs. If you prefer a pastry pie, line a dish with pastry, place the cooked mixture in, layer grated cheese on top, then cover with a pastry lid. Brush with egg, and bake in a medium to hot oven until cooked and browned. Again, basically, this is a recipe to adapt to your own choice of ingredients, whatever you have to hand.

Mincemeat Cake

This is a lovely, easy recipe and so good for using up jars of mincemeat once Christmas is over. It is actually a very good cake to make for Christmas, if you are not a fan of the heavy fruit variety. This one can still be covered in marzipan and iced but, of course, needn't be made in advance.

Ingredients

6oz margarine, 6oz light brown sugar, 3 eggs, 9oz self-raising flour, 1 teaspoon baking powder, 1 standard jar mincemeat, 2oz sultanas, milk to mix. You could add 1 teaspoon mixed spice, but this is optional.

Method

Cream together the margarine and sugar. Gradually beat in the eggs. Fold in flour, then the mincemeat and sultanas. Add milk if necessary to get a dropping consistency. Pour into a greased and lined 8-inch-deep cake tin, and bake at gas mark 4 or 160 fan for about 1 to 1½ hours.